Twayne's English Authors Series

EDITOR OF THIS VOLUME

Arthur F. Kinney

University of Massachusetts

Thomas More

TEAS 247

Hans Holbein portrait of
Thomas More

THOMAS MORE

By JUDITH P. JONES
Auburn University at Montgomery

TWAYNE PUBLISHERS
A DIVISION OF G. K. HALL & CO., BOSTON

Published in 1979 by Twayne Publishers,
A Division of G. K. Hall & Co.
All Rights Reserved

Printed on permanent/durable acid-free paper and bound
in the United States of America

First Printing

Library of Congress Cataloging in Publication Data

Jones, Judith P
Thomas More.

(Twayne's English authors series ; TEAS 247)
Bibliography: p. 158 - 62
Includes index.
1.   More, Thomas, Sir, Saint, 1478 - 1535—Criticism
and interpretation.   I.   Kinney, Arthur F., 1933 -
PR2322.J6 1979   828'.2'09   78-13021
ISBN 0-8057-6711-8

For Beth and Charles

Contents

About the Author

Judith P. Jones received her B.A. from Hollins College and her M.A. and Ph.D. from Auburn University. She is now an Associate Professor in the Department of English at Auburn University at Montgomery. She has published numerous articles on Renaissance and Modern writers including Thomas More, Philip Roth, Joyce Carol Oates, and Sylvia Plath. She is the author of the Thomas More bibliography in the *Recent Studies Series* published in *English Literary Renaissance* and is writing a study of the novels of Philip Roth.

Preface

More than any other single figure, Thomas More demonstrates in his life and his writings the unique character of the great age of change in which he lived; his life and his works have an integrality rare in history. Yet, to most students, More is known in only the most fragmentary way: for some he is the author of the *Utopia*; others know he was executed for opposing Henry VIII's divorce; sometimes now he is recognized as the hero of Robert Bolt's popular play, *A Man for All Seasons*. Similarly historians have often viewed More's diverse accomplishments in segments and thus found him paradoxical. He has been depicted as a man who wrote a radical book of reform and then became rigidly conservative, who advocated political and religious freedom but persecuted reformers for their beliefs, who wrote brilliantly and wisely but was unable, or unwilling, to save himself from King Henry's petulant wrath. It is all too easy to explain More's behavior in terms of age and see in him that familiar metamorphosis which turns the optimistic liberality of youth into the frightened conservatism of middle age. The appeal of such an interpretation is that it relieves us of the burden of trying to understand the complexity of More's personality, the ironic orientation that permeated his profoundly religious view of life, and the vast changes occuring in the world in which he lived.

But it was the continuity of More's character rather than its fragmentation that led Bolt to see More as a man heroic for the modern world because of his "adamantine sense of his own self." Bolt chose him not so much for his sainthood as for his selfhood and suggests that though we may no longer understand the saint, we still admire a man totally committed to his own sense of who he was. For Bolt, it was that commitment which Thomas More valued more than life. Although Bolt is concerned with More the man rather than More the writer, the quotation from which he takes his title links the two—describing More as a man of wit, learning, merriment, and humility. Erasmus also describes him as a man of literary, intellectual, and moral breadth, often regretting that More was not able to devote himself totally to scholarship and writing.

More's personality is of course complex, but it is neither contradictory nor confused. What we know of his early life suggests that his interests were diverse from the beginning. He wanted to study everything—theology, law, the classics. He wanted to marry, but the religious life also appealed to him; he was attracted to action as well as to contemplation, to secular politics and to the Church, to mysticism and to humanism. Yet, his is not a story of increasing disjunction but of increasing integration and self-expression. The process of maturation and integration becomes apparent when we look at More's works chronologically, especially in terms of his youthful conflicts and goals.

The purpose of this book is to survey More's writing and show the extent to which it demonstrates his intellectual and spiritual development. Chapter 1 is a brief account of the facts of More's life. Chapter 2 discusses the years of early maturity and increasing involvement in the active life—of family, government, and humanism. This is the period of two of More's most important books, the *Utopia* and the *History of Richard III*. Chapter 3 is a consideration of the polemical works, which reveal More's theological concerns and his commitment to the Catholic Church. Chapter 4 analyzes the mystical strain in More's thought as it appears in the prison writings; it includes an analysis of the prison masterpiece, the *Dialogue of Comfort*. Chapter 5 is an assessment of More's historical and literary significance. In studying More's literary career—as humanist, polemicist, and devotional writer—we see the unfurling of the qualities inherent in his personality. As a young man, More wanted to be a statesman, a churchman, a scholar, a writer, a contemplative. By the end of his life he had become all these things.

Thomas More was canonized in 1935. In the same year, R. W. Chambers published his comprehensive biography of More. Since then there has been something of a "More Renaissance." The St. Thomas More Project at Yale University has begun publishing scholarly editions of the *Complete Works of Thomas More*. And in 1962 the Association *Amici Thomae Mori* was established to bring together the wide range of persons interested in More and Morean scholarship. The *Amici*, under the leadership of Abbé Germain Marc'hadour, publishes the quarterly bulletin *Moreana*, "to provide a forum for research and discussion about the world of Saint Thomas More." My book is obviously indebted to the work of R. W. Chambers and to recent scholarship, especially by the writers of the

Preface

Yale *Complete Works,* and the members of the Association *Amici Thomae Mori.* I owe much to Professors Ward Allen and Richard Marius and to Abbé Germain Marc'hadour; their personal and scholarly support has been invaluable to me. Thanks are also due to the Folger Shakespeare Library, the Newberry Library, and Auburn University; I am particularly grateful to the Newberry Library for a fellowship that enabled me to use its collection during the summer of 1974 and to Auburn University at Montgomery for a grant which facilitated my work in More bibliography. I wish to express my appreciation to Judith Rigby and Andrew Green for their endless help with the manuscript and to Therese Ford for her care and patience in typing it. I am indebted to all the Twayne staff but especially to Arthur F. Kinney for his wise and conscientious editing. I gratefully acknowledge permission granted by Yale University Press to quote "A Godly Meditation" from *Thomas More's Prayer Book.* For More's English works I have used either the 1557 edition or reliable modern editions. Where the Latin is translated, I acknowledge the source of the translation.

JUDITH P. JONES

Chronology

1477 or 1478	Thomas More born February 6 or 7 in London.
ca. 1490	Becomes a page in the home of John Morton, Archbishop of Canterbury and Lord Chancellor.
ca. 1492	Enters Oxford.
ca. 1494	Goes to New Inn to study law.
1496	Admitted to Lincoln's Inn.
1499	Meets Erasmus.
1501	Resides in or near the Charterhouse of London. Admitted to the Bar.
ca. 1503	Composes the Nine Pageants, "Ode on the Death of Elizabeth of York," and verses for the *Book of Fortune*.
1504	Elected to Parliament.
1504 or 1505	Marries Jane Colt.
1505	Sends *The Life of John Picus* to Joyeuce Leigh as a New Year's gift; ca. September, daughter Margaret born.
1506	April, completes the translation of Lucian. Daughter Elizabeth born.
1507	Daughter Cecily born.
1508	Visits Louvain and Paris. Son John born at end of 1508 or early in 1509.
1510	Elected to Parliament; made Under-Sheriff of London; ca. 1510, *Life of John Picus* printed for the first time.
1511	ca. July-August, Jane Colt More dies; ca. August-September, marries the widow Alice Middleton.
1515	Embassy to Flanders.
1515 1516	Writes *Utopia*. It is finished by the summer of 1516 and printed in Louvain.
1517	Evil May Day riot. Embassy to Calais. More joins the King's council. *Utopia* printed in Paris. Luther presents his theses at Wittenberg.
1518	*Utopia* printed at Basel in March and November.

Epigrammata printed with the third edition of *Utopia*. The *Letter to Germanus Brixius* printed. Works on the *History of Richard III* between 1514 and 1518.

1520   At Bruges. December, the *Epigrammata* printed separately by John Froben.

1521   Knighted. Becomes Under-Treasurer. Embassy to Bruges and Calais.

1522   Works on *The Four Last Things* with Margaret.

1523   April, elected Speaker of the House of Commons; ca. end of May, *Responsio ad Lutherum* printed under the name of Ferdinand Baravellus. September, *Responsio* reprinted under name of Gulielmus Rosseus.

1524   Becomes High Steward of Oxford University.

1525   Becomes High Steward of Cambridge University. Made Chancellor of the Duchy of Lancaster.

ca. 1526   Writes the *Letter to John Bugenhagen*.

1527   Embassy to France.

1528   March 7, Tunstall commissions More to defend the Church in English.

1529   Publication of the *Dialogue concerning Tyndale*, the first of More's English polemical books. Embassy to Cambrai. September, publication of *The Supplication of Souls*. October 25, More becomes Lord Chancellor.

1531   February 11, the clergy acknowledges Henry "Supreme Head of the Church in England."

1532   Publication of *The Confutation of Tyndale's Answer*, I - III. May 16, resigns the Chancellorship. December 7, writes *Letter to John Frith*.

1533   April, publication of the *Apology of Sir Thomas More, Knight*. October, publication of *The Debellation of Salem and Bizance*. December, completion of the *Answer to the Poisoned Book*. Publication of *Confutation of Tyndale's Answer*, IV - VIII.

1534   Examined by the King's Council. March, Act of Succession passed. April 13, at Lambeth Palace, refuses the oath. April 17, imprisoned in the Tower of London.

1534 -
1535   Writes the *Dialogue of Comfort*, the treatises on the Passion, prison devotions.

1535   July 1, trial and condemnation. July 6, More beheaded on Tower Hill.

CHAPTER 1

Britain's Genius

I T is not surprising that Robert Bolt's play *A Man for All
Seasons* removed Thomas More (1477 - 1535) from the relative
obscurity of the history books and made him a modern hero. More
lived in an exciting but troubled age. Not unlike the present, it was
a time characterized by the confusion and fragmentation that accompanies rapid change. He was born in the traditional,
hierarchical, and Church-centered Middle Ages; by the time he
died, nationalism, religious revolution, and an immense expansion
in knowledge and experience had shattered the security of a universal system of values. John Colet, a scholar himself, called More the
one genius of Britain;[1] he was a scholar, statesman, theologian, and
ascetic. But the most profound expression of his genius lay in his
ability to transcend, in his life and in his writings, the great conflicts
of the age in which he lived. Our unsettled world naturally turns to
one who survived personal and social disorientation with intergrity.

Thomas More—who was born during the reign of Edward IV, was a
child in the time of Richard III, and grew up under Henry VII—saw
the development of the Renaissance in England. Henry VII established the economically and politically stable milieu that made possible
the expansion of ideas and scholarship in the sixteenth-century
England. But it was not until his son Henry VII came to the throne
(1509) that the New Learning, or humanism, flourished. The young
king encouraged scholars like Thomas More until the events of the
1520s brought many of them into disagreement with his attitude
toward the Catholic Church. Thus the first phase of the English
Renaissance was brief and ended abruptly with the reorganization of
the Church. By the time of More's death (July 6, 1535), the
Renaissance had ended and the Reformation had begun. As we shall
see, More's political and literary careers are intricately intertwined
with the events that define this revolutionary period of history.

I *Apprenticeship*

Thomas More was born on February 6, 1477 or 1478,[2] the son of John More, a prosperous London lawyer. We know little of More's early childhood, only that his mother died when he was young and that he attended St. Anthony's school. But we have some detailed descriptions of the formative years following his twelfth or thirteenth birthday; he spent this important period as a page in the household of John Morton, Lord Chancellor of England, Archbishop of Canterbury, and later to be Cardinal. At that time, it was customary to send promising boys, still too young for the university, into the households of educated men to further their training and experience. It may have been in Morton's home that More first felt the necessity of choosing between two desirable careers—one in the Church, the other in public life—for here he was exposed early to the greatest ecclesiastical and political minds of the realm. But Morton must have decided that his young friend's career was to be in the Church, for after having More in his home for two years, he placed him at Oxford, the usual training ground for aspiring churchmen. There he studied Latin and perhaps Greek. Less than two years later, however, he was at an Inn of Chancery studying law. Probably at the insistence of his father, More was now being prepared for a secular career. Nicholas Harpsfield, one of his early biographers, suggests that although More was inclined to stay at Oxford to pursue theology and the humanities, John More insisted that his son enter his profession.[3] The choices made by More, or for him, at this point largely determined that the accomplishments of his early manhood would be in public affairs rather than in the Church or the university.

More was in his early twenties and still at the Inns of Law when Erasmus paid his first visit to England and further challenged his studies with the humanist's enthusiasm for classical literature. While in England, Erasmus spent time at Oxford, where he met John Colet and the other Oxford scholars who, along with himself and More, were to form the nucleus of humanist scholarship in England for the next thirty years. The meeting between Erasmus and Thomas More began a friendship which would last their lifetimes—despite their clearly oppositional interpretations of some of the events of the Reformation—and enhance the spiritual and literary development of both men.

A few years after his meeting with Erasmus, More accepted an invitation to deliver a series of public lectures on Augustine's *De Civitate Dei* (The City of God). According to Harpsfield, More continued his legal and classical studies while working on the lectures, which were greatly admired by an audience that included some of the most learned and important men in London.[4] Yet More continued to progress in the law and by 1501 had been admitted to the Bar of London and was himself lecturing at Furnival's Inn. While studying and practicing law, More lived in a Carthusian monastery where he gave himself to devotion and prayer, "religiously lyvinge there, without vowe, about iiij^{er} yeares."[5] Undoubtedly the Carthusian influence strengthened an innate asceticism which found full expression only in the last years of More's life. Early accounts of his education and youth suggest the tension created by conflicting political, scholarly, and spiritual inclinations. The remarkable thing is not the conflict, which so clearly reflects the age in which More lived, but what he was able to accomplish in spite of, or perhaps because of, it. He had a varied and long political career, eventually becoming Lord Chancellor; he produced the literary masterpiece of the early English Renaissance; he defended the Catholic Church against the Lutherans with massive polemical writings; and he approached the personal perfection of the Christian mystic. Perhaps rather than being exhausted by conflicting demands, More was stimulated by them.

Between 1501 and 1505, the young Thomas More must have made some decisions in favor of a secular profession, for by 1505 he had married Jane Colt and begun to accept the responsibilities that led him into politics. In 1504 he was elected to the House of Commons, where he immediately earned the displeasure of King Henry VII in a conflict that foreshadows his tragic disagreement with Henry's son. The king was entitled to a grant to alleviate the cost of the marriage of his daughter Margaret and the knighting of his deceased son Arthur. But when Henry requested a large sum, More, then twenty-seven or twenty-eight years old, opposed him and succeeded in getting the grant reduced. According to William Roper, More's son-in-law and earliest biographer, after Parliament had overthrown the king's plans, a member of the king's privy chamber "brought word to the kinge . . . that a beardles boy had disapointed all his purpose." Both Roper and a later writer, Thomas Stapleton, tell of More's opposition to the king and the threats he received because of it.[6] Although these accounts of More's courage and the vengefulness of Henry VII may be exaggerated, Roper's facts are usually correct. He says that More had to retire politically until the king's death five years later, during which time he considered the danger to himself so great that he feared it might be necessary for him to leave England.[7] We know that in 1508 More visited the Universities of Paris and Louvain, perhaps intending to live abroad for a while.[8]

During this time, More established his family at Bucklersbury in London and fathered four children: Margaret, born in 1505; Elizabeth, in 1506; Cecily, in 1507; and John, in 1508.[9] But despite increasing professional and personal responsibilities, he did not abandon his spiritual and scholarly concerns. He supposedly wore a hair shirt all his life and at times scourged himself with whips and knotted cords to subdue the desires of the body.[10] A letter from More to John Colet written on October 23, 1504, shows him continuing his studies with other English humanists.[11]

II *Humanism*

In brief, Renaissance humanism was a cultural and educational movement that began in Italy in the fourteenth century and gradually spread to other European countries. It emphasized the intensive study of Greek and Latin language and literature and held that the best way to learn to write and speak well was through the study of the ancients. Philosophically, it stressed the importance of the moral development of the individual, the effects of learning on morality, and the uniqueness of man.[12]

Thomas More began writing early; we have a number of poems from his boyhood and early manhood. Although many of the extant English poems were not published until 1557 when More's nephew, William Rastell, printed his black-letter edition of More's English works, a collection of his Latin epigrams appeared in 1518 in an edition of the *Utopia* which included poems by More, William Lily, and Erasmus. The *Epigrammata* were popular enough to be reprinted in 1518 and again in 1520, this time separate from the *Utopia* and with significant authorial revisions.

When Erasmus made his second trip to England in 1505, he found in More an able partner for translating into Latin some of the dialogues of the Greek poet Lucian. In 1506 the Parisian printer Badius Ascensius published the translations. The work with Lucian allowed More to practice his Green and to experiment with irony, satire, and dialogue, all of which became important techniques in his own mature style.

More's English translation of the Latin *Life of John Picus Earl of Mirandula,* completed in 1505 but not published until 1510, was also important to his personal and literary development. The book is a translation of the *Life of John Picus* written by Picus's nephew, John Francis. Tradition has it that, when More married and chose the active over the contemplative life, he took as his model John Picus, an Italian layman and scholar who, like himself, had considered a life of religious contemplation.[13]

So the years between 1504 and 1509 were philosophically and intellectually productive for More; he was making the major choices of his life and getting the training that would make him England's outstanding humanist. And, although he was politically inactive until after the death of Henry VII, he continued to progress in his profession. Thus, when Henry VIII became king in April of 1509, Thomas More was on the brink of a maturity during which he would occupy the highest governmental office in the land and write the first "Utopia" in the English language as well as the first historical biography.

At the beginning of Henry VIII's reign, More was a successful lawyer earning a comfortable income. In 1510, he was again chosen to sit in the House of Commons, this time as a representative of the city of London. That same year he became one of the two under-sheriffs of the city. An under-sheriff's job, which was important but not time-consuming, involved advising the sheriff and the court on certain legal matters. So, for a while, More was to prosper without sacrificing the time he wanted for his family and his studies. As we shall see, modern scholars often disagree with More's early Catholic biographers concerning More's attitude toward his political career. Still, it seems likely that the early writers are correct in saying that, at this point, More was reluctant to give up a pleasant combination of prosperity, service, and leisure to become involved in royal politics.[14] Nevertheless, his reputation for success and honesty attracted the king's attention, and in 1515 he was sent to Flanders with his fellow humanist, Cuthbert Tunstall, to negotiate a commercial treaty with Prince Charles of Castile. The mission, which was to have lasted two months, lasted six, causing More to complain to Erasmus of the economic and domestic inconveniences of such a long absence from home.[15] Still, More was not altogether unhappy with the trip to Flanders; for, while there, he enjoyed the company of Tunstall and two of the outstanding humanists of the Low Countries, Jerome Busleyden and Peter Giles. And it was there, inspired at least in part by the spirit of international humanism, that More began the *Utopia*. Upon his return More was offered a royal pension for his services, one which he refused—fearing to divide his loyalties between the king and the city of London.

In May of 1517, More was much involved in the unpleasant events of "Evil May Day," a demonstration against foreign laborers, started half in jest by a handful of London apprentices. The demonstration got out of control, and those involved were charged with violating the safe-conduct of foreigners. On May 4 about forty of them were hanged; the rest of the demonstrators were saved from execution by a plea from the officials of London represented by Thomas More. Another incident of that same year attracted the king's attention. More was representing the Pope in a case against the king, who claimed the forfeiture of a ship arriving at Southhampton. Roper gives the following account of the legal proceedings and their aftermath:

Where Sir Thomas Moore not onlye déclared to thembassador the whole effecte of all their opinions, But also, in defens [of] the Popes side, argued so learnedly himself, that both was the foresaid forfeyture to the Pope restored, and himself amonge all the hearers, for his vpright and comendable demeanor therein, so greatly renowned, that for no intreaty wold the king from thenceforth be induced any longer to forbeare his service.[16]

On August 26, More was commissioned to make another diplomatic trip for the king, this time to Calais to negotiate an agreement between French and English merchants. In a letter to Erasmus dated October 25, he again indicates his distaste for that sort of business,[17] perhaps magnified now because commercial affairs were so closely connected with the chaotic foreign policy of Henry VIII and his ruthless Lord Chancellor, Thomas Wolsey. More returned to London at Christmas to begin a steady rise in the king's service. Despite some reservations, he probably came to court with a degree of optimism. An international peace had been established, and he, like other humanists, continued to hope that Henry's interest in scholarship would combine with political stability to produce the Golden Age of peace and learning.[18]

The years between 1515 and 1518 mark the beginning of More's political prominence and the peak of his productivity as a humanist writer; later he would devote his energies first to the state, then to the defense of the Church, and finally to the contemplation of God and death. But never again would he be so involved in literature and scholarship. He began the *Utopia* in Flanders in 1515, writing

Book II and parts of Book I there; upon his return to London he finished Book I, and in September 1516 he sent the manuscript to Erasmus for publication.[19] The book was printed three times during the next four years. Also, by 1518, More had written his *History of Richard III*, although it remained unfinished and was not published until after his death.

At this point, More's political career had not yet begun to interfere with his humanist activities. He continued his Greek and Latin studies and developed friendships with many English and Continental humanists. A letter written to Oxford University in 1518 delineates his humanist philosophy of education—that a combination of classical and theological training produces superior intellectual, spiritual, and moral development in the individual and that Christian wisdom and virtue are increased by exposure to the best minds of the ancients.[20] More practiced this philosophy in his own home, where he established a school for the girls and boys of his extended family. He had in his school not only his own four children but at various times many others, including his foster daughter, Margaret Giggs; his stepdaughter, Alice Middleton; his ward, Anne Cresacre; John Clement, William Roper, and Giles Heron. The students learned Greek, Latin, Logic, Philosophy, Theology, Mathematics, and Astronomy. More expected high quality in their work and carefully directed the school by letter when he was away from home. Since many of the students were girls, his letters often defend the education of women, insisting that learning increases virtue in women, that women are often as competent as men, and when they are not, learning will help mitigate their inferiority. More's letters to the children and their tutors describe his goals for their education—it should first teach virtue and wisdom, then language and the liberal studies, thereby making the students both better Christians and better scholars.[21]

The school proved a successful experiment and set a precedent for educating women. Margaret More Roper became an accomplished language scholar and translated for publication Erasmus's *Treatise on the Pater Noster*. Her daughter Mary Basset was equally proficient in Latin and translated into English her grandfather's Latin treatise, "De Tristitia Christi." Margaret Giggs was a scholar of Greek, medicine, and mathematics; John Clement, her husband, became a lecturer in Rhetoric and a reader in Greek at Oxford and by 1528 was the Court Physician; William Roper was a successful lawyer as well as More's first biographer.

III *Politics*

By 1519, Thomas More's major period of humanistic productivity
was ending; the next twelve years would see the culmination of his
political career. By 1517, More was a member of the king's Council,
and in July 1518 he resigned his position with the city of London in
order to commit himself fully to the king's service. From 1517 he
was often involved in Henry's diplomatic affairs; in 1520 and 1521,
his ambassadorial travels on behalf of the king and the English
merchants afforded him several meetings with Erasmus, one at
Calais and two at Bruges.[22] But by then hostilities involving
England, France, and Spain had ended for good the humanists'
dream of a new Golden Age. Furthermore, Europe was feeling the
disruptive effects of the Reformation and at home Henry was growing restless over the succession.

More's personal fortunes, however, were still rising. He was appointed Under-Treasurer and Chancellor of the Exchequer in May
1521; the Under-Treasurership brought responsibilities and a high
salary. More, now Sir Thomas, was increasingly involved in affairs
of international diplomacy. His position was a complex one when in
1523 he was chosen speaker of the House of Commons, for his commitment to the crown made it necessary that he be involved in
financing the European wars to which he objected. On one occasion
Wolsey requested 800,000 pounds. The Commons were un-
cooperative although apparently More did what he could to fulfill
his obligation to the king. Eventually some money was granted, but
Roper indicates that Wolsey blamed More for the temperament of
the Commons.[23] Yet More must have continued in the king's favor.
In 1525 he received additional recognition, becoming the
Chancellor of the Duchy of Lancaster and High Steward of Cambridge; he was already High Steward of Oxford. He resigned the
Under-Treasurership when he became the Chancellor of the Duchy
of Lancaster but continued his diplomatic duties and became one of
the four Council members to be in constant attendance to the king.
More participated in the negotiations with France from 1525
through 1527 and was among the signers of the Franco-English
agreement of April 1527. But early in 1529 word reached England
that France and Spain were making, at Cambrai, a military and
political agreement which would isolate England. However, by
now, Henry and Wolsey had become so obsessed with their
attempts to secure a divorce for the king that they managed to un-
derestimate the seriousness of the situation for some months. Final-

ly, in June, More, Tunstall, and Dr. William Knight were sent to
Cambrai, but there was little they could do for England at this point
other than reestablish trade relations with the Low Countries and
Spain. Yet the peace made there in August 1529 lasted fourteen
years, and his role in it was so important to More that he included it
among the accomplishments listed in his epitaph: "In that place he
witnessed, in the capacity of ambassador, to his great joy, the
renewal of a peace treaty between the supreme monarchs of
Christendom and the restoration of a long-desired peace to the
world."[24]

Cambrai, which represented the complete failure of English
foreign policy, was the final blow to Wolsey's career. His oppressive
political methods and his attempts to support wars by taxation had
alienated English people of all classes. And his failure to secure
from the Pope the annulment of Henry's marriage to Catherine had
lost him the support of the king. Wolsey's fall was complete when,
in October, he resigned the Lord Chancellorship; immediately it
was presented to Thomas More, who must have suspected that if he
became Chancellor the issue of Henry's divorce would lead to conflict between himself and the king.[25] Perhaps, however, he was
obliged to accept the office once it was offered, and apparently
Henry had assured him at some point that as Chancellor he would
not be made to betray his conscience.[26]

More served as Lord Chancellor for two and a half years; finally
it was not the divorce so much as Henry's conflict with the Church
that forced him to resign. The king launched a campaign which he
thought would either force the Pope to agree to the divorce or allow
him to be divorced without the permission of the Pope. On
February 11, 1531, he succeeded in getting the English clergy to
acknowledge him "their singular protector, only and supreme Lord,
and so far as the law of Christ allows, even Supreme Head." Henry
pressed his advantage and by May 15, 1532, he had complete control of the clergy, finally making them subject to him alone rather
than jointly to both him and the Pope. From this point, Henry was
free to do as he pleased; having placed himself at the top of the
Church hierarchy in England, he controlled both Church and State.
The portents for the future were clear; the next day, More resigned
the Chancellorship, claiming ill health. We know from his letters to
friends[27] that he was suffering from a heart condition, but undoubtedly the impossibility of his political position hastened his
retirement and aggravated the illness.

The years that More spent in political service pose some difficulty for modern scholars since his earliest biographers, Roper, Harpsfield, and Stapleton—all Catholic apologists—and even his most thorough twentieth-century biographer, R. W. Chambers, neglect this period in order to emphasize the dramatic last years of More's life. Until recently, very little has been known of the time during which More devoted most of his energies to serving the king. His major biographers consistently depict him as a man without worldly ambition drawn into government against his will—either out of a sense of duty or because of irresistible pressure from the king. According to Roper, More tried to avoid political service; and when he finally accepted it, he did so from a completely selfless desire to serve "god, the prince, and the realme."[28] Harpsfield is more precise than Roper in describing Thomas More's distaste for his governmental jobs: "He of his owne selfe and of nature neither desired nor well lyked to be intricated with Princes affaires."[29] Harpsfield insists that More accepted the Chancellorship unwillingly, out of a sense of responsibility to his country and a reluctance to insult the king, who "so highly and entierly fauored and loued him."[30] Stapleton insists upon More's utter indifference to "honors and wealth" but hints at a possible motive for his involvement in royal politics when he says: "Although, then, life at Court was not in itself attractive to More, yet he took some little pleasure in it in so far as it was a school of goodness and piety, as it certainly was during the first twenty years of Henry's reign."[31] Finally, he came to hate what he had never loved. Chambers follows Stapleton and Erasmus in suggesting that More was willing to enter the king's service because he believed the young Henry would foster the humanists' ideals of peace and learning.[32] And according to Chambers, More really had no choice but to accept the Chancellorship when it was offered: "Once he had entered the King's service, he was no longer a free man."[33]

Historians are now, however, beginning to examine the years between 1515 and 1532 more objectively in terms of the events of More's life. And they are trying to answer the same questions that troubled the earlier writers: Why did More join the king's Council in the first place, and why did he accept the Chancellorship, a position fraught with moral and physical danger for him?

Professor G. R. Elton has looked closely at More's political career and made a substantial contribution to our understanding of this phase of his life.[34] Elton points out the disparity between the traditional image of More's distaste for civil service and the facts of his political career—More worked hard in government for almost twenty years. Elton sees the apparent regret in the More-Erasmus correspondence as conventional and largely an expression of Erasmus's attitudes rather than More's. He concludes; "There really is no evidence that he [More] lived twelve years against the grain."[35] Elton describes More's rise in the government as gradual—the result of the normal ambition of a civil servant who accepts opportunities as they arise. But he notes that before 1529, although More did "well enough" financially, none of the positions he held gave him primary administrative responsibility or political power. Elton sees More during these years engaged predominantly in two kinds of activities—attending to diplomatic affairs and acting as a kind of informal secretary to Henry VIII. It is to his skill and service in the latter occupation that Elton attributes More's political status. Wolsey and others recognized More's position at the heart of the king's court from 1519 through 1526.

John J. Scarisbrick, another contemporary historian, thinks More served specifically as an intermediary between Henry and Wolsey; he sees More during these years being advanced by both men because their policies required someone each could trust to communicate between the "courts" of King and Lord Chancellor. Scarisbrick even speculates that "More had immersed himself in royal service in the first place" because he believed in Wolsey's ability and desire to produce reform at home and peace abroad.[36] According to Scarisbrick, More's job as "spare secretary" made him pivotal to the power structure of the 1520s. Although this position must have given More some authority and influence, neither Elton or Scarisbrick suggests that it gave him power at the level of policymaking or administration, and Elton says that it was because the position failed to satisfy More's vast ability and his sincere desire to serve that he threw himself into the Lutheran controversy with such energy.[37]

Elton and Scarisbrick depict More's early years of service to the king as unspectacular and unsatisfying, but they view his actions and motives from a perspective different from that of his earlier biographers. And both offer explanations to the troublesome questions which surround More's accepting the Chancellorship in the midst of the king's battle with the Church. Elton denies two ideas prevalent in More's biography concerning the Chancellorship—that More had no choice but to accept and that the king had promised More, before he took office, that he would not involve him in the problems surrounding the "great matter" of his marriage. Elton thinks that More and Bishop John Fisher were at the center of a conspiracy designed to thwart the king's plans with relationship to the Church and the divorce. He attributes More's secrecy in opposition to his desire to be as useful as possible. But he shows More in the Council actively opposing the king's efforts to strip the clergy of its power. More took the dangerous job then because "he hoped to use his office, as best he might, to stand guard over the things in which he believed: the orthodox faith and the liberties of the Church."[38] Any possibility of serving his purposes ended in May 1532 with the emasculation of the clergy.

Scarisbrick understands More's Chancellorship in terms of his commitment to humanism rather than to the Church. He sees More's decision as an extension of the economic and political ambition that had characterized his governmental career all along, but also as a final attempt to bring about the kinds of domestic reforms he had described in the *Utopia*: "It was Catholic humanism's last chance in England."[39]

These two studies suggest a commonness of purpose and mind between the man who wrote *Utopia* in 1515 and the man who became Lord Chancellor in 1529. More must have been making a decision about public service while writing *Utopia*. No doubt he did it with all the pragmatism and clear-sightedness of his Utopian namesake who argues that the philosopher can serve his king only if he adopts a practical, indirect, and tactful approach to counsel. This kind of statesman serves as best he can and accomplishes whatever is possible: he does not abandon his ship in a storm because he cannot control the winds; what he cannot turn to good he makes as little bad as possible.[40] More seems to have applied this "utopian" philosophy from the beginning of his political career and up until the moment of his resignation.

More's letters of this period are full of regrets that he had so little time for scholarship and correspondence. But his commitment to humanist ideals did not end when his political career began; he continued to encourage his friends and to correspond with them when he could. His correspondence, though slim during these years, includes letters to Erasmus, Germanus Brixius, William Budé, Conrad Goclenius, Francis Cranvelt, John Cochlaeus, and to the students in his home. His political activities brought him into contact with other English scholars in public positions, men like Cuthbert Tunstall, John Fisher, and Richard Pace.

In 1520 More's *Epigrammata* were reprinted; in 1521 the sixth edition of Erasmus's and More's translations of Lucian appeared; and More's translation of Lucian's *Menippus* was printed separately in 1522. In 1524 Richard Hyrde, a humanist and tutor to More's children, wrote a preface to Margaret More Roper's translation of Erasmus's *Pater Noster,* published in that year. The preface, obviously influenced by More, advocated scholarly education for women. Yet these were not happy years for the humanists, divided by wars and the increasing conflicts of the Reformation.

IV *The Church*

Though the years of political service marked a decline in More's humanist activities, they gave him an opportunity to express his absolute commitment to the Church. More was involved in the Reformation debate almost from the time it began. Martin Luther declared his ninety-five theses on October 31, 1517; in March 1518 Erasmus sent More a copy of them.[41] We do not know More's immediate response; but both More and Henry seem to have been disturbed by the Lutheran heresy from its inception. Henry was concerned enough to begin writing against Luther immediately.[42] By 1520 Luther's books were being generally circulated in England, and in the early 1520s Cambridge and Oxford became centers of interest in "Lutheranism" and produced the first generation of English Protestants, among them Thomas Bilney, Robert Barnes, Hugh Latimer, Thomas Cranmer, and William Tyndale. By May 1521 official opposition had become so great that Luther's books were burned at St. Paul's Cross in London. In July, Henry published his *Assertio Septem Sacramentorum* (Assertion of the Seven Sacraments), refuting Luther's attack on the sacramental system and upholding the authority of the Church. Luther responded with *Contra Henricum Regem Angliae* (Against King Henry of England), an abusive reply which set the tone for much of the subsequent debate between the Catholic and Lutheran polemicists. Henry immediately turned the dispute over to Thomas More, who was in a better position than the king to answer to Luther's vulgar and violent book. More replied with his *Responsio ad Lutherum* (Answer to Luther), printed in May 1523 and bearing the pseudonym Ferdinandus Baravellus. It was withdrawn from circulation, revised, and reissued in September under the name of Gulielmus Rosseus. Several years later, More wrote a long polemical letter, also in Latin, to the humanist-reformer John Bugenhagen. The letter was apparently never sent to Bugenhagen and not printed until 1568.

More's career as a polemicist did not, however, begin in earnest until 1528 when Cuthbert Tunstall, now Bishop of London, asked him to defend the Church in English in order to fortify the vernacular reader against the increasingly troublesome Lutheran heresies.[43] At once More began work on his first English polemical book. As his political position became more complicated the quality of his writing deteriorated, but this first book, the *Dialogue concerning Tyndale*, is a lively dialogue that compares favorably with the *Utopia* and the later *Dialogue of Comfort*. In it a young man influenced by Lutheranism engages in a debate with a wise spokesman for Catholicism, More himself. The book was first published in June 1529, a little over a year after Tunstall instructed him to begin. More's editor, William Rastell, says that it was "made in 1528," indicating that it was begun immediately, although at the time More was much involved in activities of state. The vigorous dialogue and the humorous characterization of the two opponents reflect More's high spirits and optimism; he seemed to be renewed by the prospect of defending the faith at a time when his official duties must have been frustrating and discouraging. But the next book, *The Supplication of Souls*, published only a few months later, was obviously written in haste. Still, even after he became Lord Chancellor, More continued writing for the Church and by the end of 1532 had completed the first three books of his long *Confutation of Tyndale's Answer*. After his retirement from the Chancellorship, he finished the *Confutation* (1533) and wrote the *Apology* (1533), the *Debellation of Salem and Bizance* (1533), and the *Answer to the Poisoned Book* (1533).

Thomas More's defense of the Church was not, however, limited to his writings. During his years in public office More, like other Catholics, did everything he could to stop the spread of Lutheranism. From the early years of his political career, there were official attempts to punish Lutherans and Lutheran sympathizers. He or his officials confiscated and destroyed Lutheran books on several occasions. In January 1526 he directed a police foray into the Steelyard, the German merchant community of London. As a result, some unauthorized Bibles and prayer books were confiscated and several merchants imprisoned. Lutheran books, including William Tyndale's English translation of the New Testment, continued to be collected and burned in London throughout 1526, no doubt with More's approval. More also encouraged and participated in the trials of heretics.[44] Although men suspected of heresy were tried by the ecclesiastical rather than the civil courts, it was the job of the state, which More represented, to assign and implement the punishment of those found guilty. There is evidence that at least three heretics were burned while More was Chancellor, but in the *Apology* he denies the charges that he cruelly beat and tortured heretics.[45]

V *The Tower*

By the time of his retirement, More had found ways to fulfill his talents to various degrees, but there was one element in his nature that had not yet been expressed fully, one which was deeply personal and separate from the aggressive qualities which revealed themselves in service to Church and State. He had still to deal with the part of himself that he owed to God and not to any earthly institution. We first glimpse More's mystical inclinations in his youthful attraction to the life of the Carthusian monastery where, perhaps for the only time before his imprisonment, he devoted himself totally to worship, study, and meditation. More used poor health to explain his resignation from the Chancellorship, but a letter to Erasmus written only a month afterwards reveals motives deeper than either illness or political expediency: "It has been my constant wish almost since boyhood, dearest Desiderius, that some day I might enjoy the opportunity which, to my happiness, you have always had, namely, of being relieved of all public duties and eventually being able to devote some time to God alone and myself; at long last this wish has come true."[46] On the same day he wrote to his friend John Cochlaeus that he was retiring to recover his health and to devote his leisure to intellectual things and to God.[47] And in a letter to Henry VIII he thanks the king for allowing him to retire to devote the rest of his life to making "provision for my soul in the service of God."[48] More's famous epitaph for himself, which he included in another letter to Erasmus, repeats his longing "to have the last years of his life all to himself, so that he could gradually retire from the affairs of this world and contemplate the eternity of the life to come."[49] Even in prison he insists that the king has taken from him only his liberties and "done me so great good by the spirituall profytt that I trust I take therby, that amonge all his great benefites heaped vpon me so thicke, I reken vpon my faith my prisonment euen the very chief."[50]

These comments make More's goals for the last few years of his life clear. Although his son-in-law tells how in the months after his resignation More sometimes talked to his family of the spiritual matters of heaven, hell, martyrdom, and suffering for the faith,[51] it was not until he was in prison that he really had time for the kind of contemplation and solitude his letters describe. During the months immediately following his retirement he published four polemical books. And he invested much of his energy between 1533 and his incarceration in April 1534 to trying to protect himself and his family from the dangers inherent in his silent but conspicuous opposition to Henry's withdrawal from the Catholic Church.

In 1533, the king's domestic problems were resolved, at least temporarily, by the English annulment of his marriage to Catherine and the crowning of Anne Boleyn. After More's refusal to attend the coronation, Henry and his powerful secretary, Thomas Cromwell, began to harass More with spurious charges. First, despite a complete lack of evidence, Cromwell accused him of writing a book against the Articles of 1533, which justified Henry's marriage to Anne. Next, he brought the slightly more defensible charge that More was involved in the treason of Elizabeth Barton, who had been arrested for prophesying against the king's divorce. Elizabeth Barton was a serving maid in Kent who was reputed to have received divine revelations. she became a nun at Canterbury, and as the crisis over the king's marriage intensified she began to condemn his behavior and predict his downfall. She was encouraged by a group of Catherine's sympathizers and became something of a symbol of loyalty to the queen. She and some of her adherents were arrested, charged with treason, and eventually executed. More and others were accused of concealing evidence of the treason. More had talked to the Nun of Kent, as she was called, but refused to hear her on anything pertaining to the king's affairs and later wrote to her warning her against talking of such matters with others.[52] Nevertheless, when the Bill of Attainder against those involved in the nun's treason was introduced into the House of Lords, his name was included. More appealed directly to the king, who appointed a committee of four to hear him. But when he appeared before them, instead of questioning him about the Nun of Kent, they began trying to get his approval of recent events concerning the divorce.[53]

Immediately, More wrote both Cromwell and Henry in an effort to clarify his position concerning the nun, the divorce, and England's relationship to the Pope.[54] But by then Henry was determined to keep More's name on the list of those accused of concealing evidence against the nun. In the light of the facts, however, this was impossible, and when the Bill of Attainder came back to Parliament, More's name was not on it. Still, his problems with the king's "great matter" were not over, for in the same month Parliament passed an Act of Succession to be confirmed by oath. On April 12, 1534, More was summoned to appear the next day at the Palace of the Archbishop of Canterbury to take the oath. He declined it, saying that he could not reconcile it with his conscience but refusing to say why not. Presumably, he objected to the preamble to the act, which declared the invalidity of Henry's marriage to Catherine and negated the supremacy of the Pope. He was then committed to the custody of the Abbot of Westminster for four days, during which time Archbishop Cranmer suggested that More and John Fisher be allowed to swear the oath without the preamble if they would agree to keep secret the special circumstances of their signing. When the king refused this compromise, More was taken to the Tower of London, where he remained until his execution.[55]

At last, though the circumstances were far from pleasant, More had the solitude and leisure for contemplation; these months come to life in his Tower works—books, letters, and devotions that constitute a unique, very personal collection of meditative literature. More had not had much time for devotional writing before his imprisonment although he had at least begun the English "Treatise on the Passion," which he perhaps finished in the Tower. The English Tower works include "A Treatise to Receive the Blessed Body of our Lord," a number of letters, two short ballads, and More's prison masterpiece, the *Dialogue of Comfort*. There is also a Latin treatise on the Passion, "De Tristitia Christi." While Henry VIII continued his battle with the Catholic Church, More prepared himself for death. He was condemned for treason on July 1, 1535, and executed on July 6. When Erasmus heard of More's death he remembered the other friends he had lost and wrote of More in words that echo Colet's earlier description of Britain's genius: "First William Warham . . . then of late Mountjoy, and Fisher of Rochester, and Thomas More, Lord Chancellor of England, whose soul was more pure than any snow, whose genius was such as England never had—yea, and never shall have again, mother of good wits though England be."[56]

CHAPTER 2

The Humanist

THOMAS More's period of greatest literary achievement
comes early in his life (ca. 1501 - 1520) and mirrors his political
as well as his humanistic interests. The earliest extant works include
a few English poems, a selection of Latin epigrams, many of them
translations from the Greek, a Latin translation of some dialogues of
the Greek satirist Lucian, and a translation into English of the Latin
Life of John Picus, Earl of Mirandula. With the exception of some
of the epigrams all were finished before the end of 1506. By 1518,
More had published his humanist masterpiece, *Utopia,* and written
his *History of Richard III.* Also during this period he wrote to his
family and to fellow humanists a series of letters which for both
literary and historical reasons are among the most important
epistolary documents of the Renaissance. In 1522, he began the
Four Last Things, a treatise on death which seems strangely out of
place during this time of great personal and political success.

I *Early Poetry and Latin Epigrams*

The most nearly contemporaneous collection we have of More's
earliest writings is the 1557 edition which his nephew, William
Rastell, begins with sixteen pages of verse which he says More wrote
in his youth for his pastime. They include: "A meri iest how a
sergeant would learne to playe the frere," nine verses for some
tapestries in the More home, a poem commemorating the death of
Henry VII's wife, Queen Elizabeth, and some verses to be used in a
preface to the *Book of Fortune.* In the poems we see Thomas More
beginning at an early age to write good poetry, and although the
English poems are less interesting than the Latin epigrams, they
give us insights into More's early literary and philosophical concerns. We see him already a competent poet, writing in the vernacular about the events of his world. The poems reveal his in-

herent talent for dramatic and humorous narrative as well as his early preoccupation with the transience of life and fortune. The "Lamentation for the Queen" has special biographical significance because it describes the royal family which was to play such an important role in the author's life. But it is to the epigrams written over a number of years but not published until 1518 that we must turn for More's first substantial literary effort.

In March of 1518 the third edition of the *Utopia* appeared together with a selection of Latin epigrams by Thomas More, William Lily, and Erasmus.[1] The book was popular enough to be reprinted in December of the same year. In December 1520, More's *Epigrammata* were published separately with significant authorial corrections and revisions. We cannot date all of the epigrams exactly. Although traditionally historians have followed Erasmus, who said that More wrote most of them "when he was still a boy,"[2] recent scholarship dates many of the poems between 1509 and 1519, placing them in the period of More's early literary productivity but not exactly in his first youth; he would have been in his thirties at this time.[3]

Hoyt Hudson defines the Renaissance epigram as a short poem with a "witty or ingenious" climax brought about by antithesis, paradox, or punning, the effect of which is often satiric.[4] More's *Epigrammata* begin with the "Progymnasmata," a collection of eighteen epigrams translated by both William Lily and Thomas More from the *Greek Anthology*. Lily, More's friend and fellow scholar, was to become the first High Master of St. Paul's school. The "Progymnasmata" give the Greek, followed by More's and Lily's Latin translations. A number of the other epigrams are also from this well-known anthology; still others are translations or adaptations from Diogenes Laertius, Aristotle, Arsenius, and Martial. Two are renditions of English songs. But this account of More's sources still leaves over 150 poems that may be considered original.

The eighteen poems of the "Progymnasmata" are our earliest substantial indication of the ideas and problems that were to occupy More for a lifetime. They, like some of the early English poems, reflect the writer's acute awareness of the unpredictability of fortune and the omnipresent possibility of death: "Now I have reached port; Hope and Luck, farewell. You have nothing to do with me. Now make sport of others"; "Just as surely as I came on earth naked, so surely naked shall I quit it. Why do I struggle in vain, knowing as I do that death is naked?"[5]

Following the "Progymnasmata" is a collection of 253 poems by More. It begins with five poems commemorating the marriage and accession of Henry VIII, only three of which may properly be called epigrams. The first of the Henry poems, a long ode on the coronation, is an expression of the humanist's optimistic, perhaps naive, belief that the young king, "whose natural gifts have been enhanced by a liberal education," will bring to Christendom a golden age of learning and peace. From the perspective of the future we are struck by the irony of the lines that describe the wisdom, justice, and moral perfection of the man who was to behead their writer and end the short, scholarly Renaissance in England. Yet More is already aware of the dangers inherent in power and may be warning Henry when he says: "Unlimited power has a tendency to weaken good minds, and that even in the case of very gifted men"(no. 1). But the third poem insists again that Henry's reign ushers in a new Golden Age. The last of the epigrams for Henry VIII is the famous celebration of the union in Henry of the houses of York and Lancaster. Here More develops a conceit in which the two roses, symbolizing the two houses, combine to produce the best qualities of both lines in one flower, the Tudor king.

But it must have been the large number of earthy, dramatic epigrams that caused the immediate popularity of the *Epigrammata*. The poems, which abound with examples of More's genius for making satire, morality, and humor out of everyday events, range from the devotional to the satirical and treat an array of subjects including kingship, government, death, fortune, the clergy, and women. More satirizes drunkards, doctors, spendthrifts, misers, and courtiers.

The emphasis on rulership in the *Epigrammata* points to a concern that pervades More's writing and comes to life in his tragic relationship with Henry VIII. The poems on kingship vividly portray both good rulers and tyrants (no. 14, no. 21, no. 62, no. 91-94, no. 96, no. 97, no. 102, no. 103, no. 182, no. 185, no. 210, no. 211, no. 222). They create an image of the just king who is like a good father to his children or the wise head to the other parts of the body. They define pride and cruelty as the most dangerous qualities in rulers. Epigram 97 is More's most succinct portrayal of the two types of kings:

What is a good king? He is a watchdog, guardian of the flock. By his barking he keeps the wolves from the sheep. What is the bad king? He is the wolf.

Frequently the ruler is reminded that he, like other men, is governed by the laws of nature: he will suffer sleeplessness from guilt; unless he is just and wise, he will be in great danger; sleep and death render all alike, helpless. Furthermore, a number of the epigrams suggest that the writer had considered the advantages of republican government over monarchy. One says that the king will be safe only so long as he rules in the interest of his subjects (no. 102) and another that he should rule only so long as his subjects wish it (no. 103). Epigram no. 182 is a long consideration of whether a king or a senate governs best. More concludes that bad government is equally bad in both cases but that, if both are good, republican rule is preferable to monarchy because senators can influence one another and because they will be chosen by reason rather than by the chance of royal birth. And senators, unlike kings, are directly responsible to those who elect them.

The attitude toward death expressed in the epigrams is one which remains constant throughout More's life. The poems dealing with death (no. 22, no. 27, no. 28, no. 37, no. 38, no. 52, no. 57, no. 61, no. 62, no. 101, no. 159, no. 243) are dominated by several themes—that death is the great equalizer, coming to kings, slaves, and peasants alike; that it frees all from suffering; that it is foolish to value either good fortune or long life since death wipes everything out in an instant. Furthermore, it is foolish to fear death since it is inevitable but, unlike the misfortunes of life, comes only once and brings lasting peace. Epigram no. 101 suggests the analogy More establishes in the *Dialogue of Comfort* where he compares life to a prison in which we dwell under a death penalty that can be enforced at any moment: "We are all shut up in the prison of this world under sentence of death. In this prison none escapes death."

Another group of poems in the *Epigrammata* requires consideration for historical and biographical as well as literary reasons. These epigrams are the product of a controversy that developed between the French poet Germanus Brixius (or Germain de Brie) and Thomas More. The dispute began with a sea battle which took place on August 10, 1512, between the English ship *Regent* and the French *Cordelèire*. In the midst of the fighting, the *Cordelèire* exploded, causing the destruction of both ships and the drowning of many men, among them the captain of the French vessel, Herve Porzmoguer. The next year, Brixius published an epic poem, *Herveus*, celebrating the battle and romanticizing Porzmoguer's conduct. Thomas More, who resented both the slurs on English

honor and the extravagant praise of the French, responded with a
collection of epigrams for private circulation. When, a few years
later, More published the *Epigrammata*, he considered withholding
the controversial epigrams out of respect for the now peaceful
relationship between England and France. Although More wrote to
Erasmus, who was handling the publication of the poems, and asked him to consider excising the epigrams against Brixius, nine of
them appeared in the first edition.[6] The poems attack Brixius's style
as well as his biased version of the events. The following year, Brixius replied with the Latin poem *Antimorus*, in which he accuses
More of writing fantastic poetry marred by bad Latinity and verse.
And, more seriously, he suggests that his opponent had insulted the
memory of Henry VII in the poem celebrating the accession of
Henry VIII; the poem had of course been written years earlier but
was not published until 1518. More perpetuated the debate in his
Epistle to Germanus Brixius and in the 1520 edition of the *Epigrammata*, which included additional poems against the French writer.
Interestingly, however, when More reissued the epigrams, he cor-
rected some of his Latin in accordance with Brixius's criticism.
Erasmus's letters indicate that he was finally able to reconcile the
two humanists, and that they may even have met.[7]

In the *Epigrammata*, we see foreshadowed many facets of
Thomas More's literary future. Already he is a humanist scholar of
Greek and Latin, a fiction writer, a satirist, and a polemicist.

II   *The Lucianic Works*

By the time Erasmus made his second visit to England in 1505,
Thomas More was married and established in the law profession.
During the intervening years both men had studied Greek, the
knowledge of which had become essential to the educational and
cultural goals of the humanists. For part of his brief stay in
England, Erasmus may have been a guest in the More home. In any
case, the two of them spent enough time together to translate into
Latin some dialogues of the Greek poet and satirist Lucian of
Samosata (ca. 125 - 90 B.C.). By the middle of 1506 Erasmus was in
Paris arranging for the publication of the Lucianic book, a volume
containing twenty-eight dialogues translated by Erasmus and four
by Thomas More. In addition to the translations, the book included
answers by both authors to Lucian's declamation the *Tyrannicide*.
More's contribution included a dedicatory letter and Latin
translations of the dialogues *Cynicus* (The Cynic), *Menippus* (The

Descent into Hades), *Philopseudes* (The Lover of Lies), and the declamation *Tyrannicida* (The Tyrannicide), as well as his Latin answer to the *Tyrannicide*.

More's dedicatory letter to Thomas Ruthall defends the use of Greek literature and is an important document in the history of Christian humanism. More explains that he admires Lucian because he combines "delight with instruction" to expose human folly: the *Cynicus* recommends "Christian simplicity, temperance, and frugality"; the *Menippus* criticizes superstitions and the quibbling of the philosophers; the *Philopseudes* entertains with irony and humor at the same time that it decries lying. Not surprisingly, More finds it necessary to explain his attitude toward Lucian's disbelief in immortality. He insists that, regardless of his beliefs, a pagan writer can offer useful lessons and examples to Christian readers.[8]

The teaching of Greek was new at the universities in 1506, so much so that some twelve years later More was still defending it with arguments similar to the ones in the letter to Ruthall. In 1518 he wrote the directors of Oxford University encouraging them to continue teaching the ancients despite attacks from those who claimed that classical learning was inappropriate and unnecessary to the education of Christians, especially the clergy. More insists that the study of Greek and Latin benefits both laymen and clergymen because in teaching the laws of human nature and good conduct it "trains the soul in virtue." He adds: "Moreover, there are some who through knowledge of things natural (i.e., rational) construct a ladder by which to rise to the contemplation of things supernatural; they build a path to theology through philosophy and the liberal arts."[9]

The letter to Ruthall is followed by More's Latin translations of the *Cynicus*, a short debate between a cynic and his friend Lycinus. It demonstrates the cynic's belief that virtue and temperance rather than pleasure constitute true happiness. Lucian's mastery of dramatic characterization and dialogue suggest that the Greek writer may have been a model for More as he developed his own techniques for instructing and entertaining through dialogue. Lucian's cynic advocates the simple life and proves, as Hythlodaeus does in *Utopia*, that one is happiest when his needs are fulfilled simply rather than with extravagance and ornamentation. He often reminds his opponent that there is more reason for him to agree with those who think extravagance is best than with people who, like himself, choose simplicity.

The *Menippus* describes another cynic in search of the truth.

Menippus tells a friend how, disillusioned by the behavior of the gods and the conflicting views of the philosophers, he had allowed a magician to take him to Hades for an interview with the seer Tiresias, from whom he hoped to learn what kind of life is best. The dialogue creates a vivid, Dantesque view of the sinners in hell; some of them are being accused by their shadows, who have, of course, observed all their masters' good and bad deeds in life. Those found guilty of pride of wealth or position are punished with particular harshness; rich and poor alike suffer according to their past behavior. The dialogue satirizes foolishness, sin, dishonesty, and especially the human misunderstanding of Lady Fortune, who gives and takes as she pleases and inevitably takes everything at death. His consideration of Fortune leads Menippus to compare life to a stage performance at the end of which all alike must shed their costumes; More recalls this metaphor later in *The Four Last Things*, *Richard III*, and *Utopia*. Finally Menippus meets Tiresias, who, in contrast to the solemn philosophers encountered on earth, tells him that the simple, unintellectual life is the most enjoyable.

The *Philopseudes* satirizes man's enjoyment of unmotivated lies in a conversation between Philocles and his skeptical friend Tychiades, who recounts the preposterous tales he heard at a gathering of philosophers. Tychiades and Philocles are both lenient in their treatment of the fables and exaggerations of poets and patriots who are motivated by the desire to please readers and praise their homelands; but they consider those who lie for no reason to be utterly ridiculous. Tychiades concludes by reminding his friend that there is a sure antidote for lies in the sound and constant application of reason.

More's fourth Lucianic translation is a declamation rather than a dialogue. The declamation appears frequently in Greek and Roman oratory and was commonly used as an exercise for schoolboys. The *Tyrannicide* is the kind of declamation or monologue created for argumentation either in the courtroom or in imitation of the courtroom. Like the dialogue, the declamation is ideal for More because it allows the speaker, or writer, to develop a dramatic persona who may speak for himself, for the author, or for both.

Lucian's *Tyrannicide* is the defense of a man who claims to have slain the tyrant of a city. He tells how he went to the Acropolis to kill the king and, not finding him, killed the prince. He now insists that he deserves the customary reward for slaying the tyrant of a Greek city-state since the tyrant's grief at the death of his son caused him to remove the killer's sword from the prince's body and stab himself. Thus he claims to have put to death not one but two tyrants. The speech is an elaborate defense of the killer's position and a refutation of the argument that he does not deserve the reward since he did not kill the original tyrant himself. The speaker says that he planned the deaths in the way they occurred; now, having killed both the king and the strong, destructive prince, he has freed the city from an enslavement which would have lasted long after the king's death. He dramatizes his argument by stressing the success of his plan, describing his bravery and patriotism, and claiming that his only motive in asking for the reward is his desire to be honored as he deserves. He emphasizes as well the ingratitude of those who benefit from his act of liberation but refuse him the reward. The declamation ends with the assertion that the actual deed is far superior to the murder of a single tyrant.

In addition to the translations, Erasmus and More each wrote an original Latin declamation in reply to the *Tyrannicide*. In his reply, More assumes the role of the tyrannicide's opponent in a speech which demonstrates the extent to which he had already learned to combine drama and narrative with the rhetoric of the lawyer and the controversialist. In contrast to Lucian, More sets out immediately to dramatize the personalities of the two opponents. The speaker begins by disparaging his adversary, whom he accuses of malice, deceit, and braggadocio and by asserting his own disinterestedness and patriotism; he attacks the supposed tyrannicide on the grounds that he did not kill the tyrant and thus does not deserve the reward. He makes his point clear when he says: "If you had slain him, I would not complain; on the contrary I would praise and admire you, and I would be the first to vote for a reward" (95 - 97). More's spokesman has no objection to the reward itself, which he says restores the city's freedom, safety, and possessions. But he opposes it in this case because the mercy of the gods brought freedom without assistance from the tyrannicide. He insists that the old king was still the ruler since tyrants do not surrender power even to their own sons; the murder of the prince was not tyrannicide and should not be rewarded. The man may have intended to kill the king but he had no way of knowing that the king would kill himself. The speaker mocks his opponent for suggesting that willing a deed is the same as doing it and for insisting that he knew in advance what the king would do. Because it was the will of the gods that turned the man's blundering to good, it is they who are responsible. The speaker concludes by asking the jury to pardon the murderer and thank the gods for their freedom.

More's reply is longer than the declamation to which it responds because he expands the characterization of both the speaker and the opponent and uses exempla to point up the absurdity of the contrary opinion. In the Latin declamation More demonstrates his continuing concern for proper rulership and predicts the fervor and skill he will bring to his polemical defense of the Catholic Church.

As More knew they would, readers have often had difficulty understanding his interest in an atheistic Greek satirist who mocked the gods and doubted the immortality of the soul. The translations are a manifestation of More's and Erasmus's belief that the classics are a useful source of learning and morality so long as they are read in terms of Christian values and inspiration. More makes his position clear in the letter to Ruthall and in other letters of the period including those to the students and tutors in his household. Erasmus further clarifies the intentions of the Lucianic translations in his dedicatory letter to Richard Whitford. Here he says that More suggested they write the declamations in a spirit of friendly competition. He agreed, hoping to improve his Latin and encourage the schools to teach the eloquence of the ancients.[10] The translations and writing that resulted from the "competition" of More and Erasmus become, in effect, their best argument for the literary and educational merit of the *declamatio;* as is typical of him, More becomes an actor in his own argument.

III   The Life of John Picus, Earl of Mirandula

As with the *Epigrammata,* it is difficult to give an exact date to More's translation of John Francis's biography of his uncle Giovanni Pico della Mirandula, the renowned Italian Neoplatonist whose broad learning encompassed not only Latin literature and theology but Hebrew and Greek as well—and even included studies in the mysticism of the Jewish Cabala. John Picus, as More calls him, was a devout and scholarly fifteenth-century humanist who, like More, remained a layman despite inclinations toward monastic life. Picus's story would naturally have interested More because it reflected the same conflicts between the religious life, public service, and scholarship that must have dominated this period of his own life. But the influence of Picus on More was intellectual as well as personal; and, no doubt, a great deal of the Platonic influence in More comes through his study of Picus.

According to family tradition, when Thomas More decided to marry and commit himself to an active, political career rather than to a life of devotion, he took Picus as a model. Stapleton, like most of the early biographers, tries to explain why More failed to respond to the call of the strict religious life. He suggests that More may have rejected the monastery because the "religious communities had grown lax"; or perhaps God directed him toward public life in order that he might withstand the temptations and difficulties it presented. He tells how More, having decided on the secular life, "determined, therefore, to put before his eyes the example of some prominent layman, on which he might model his life. He called to mind all who at that period, either at home or abroad, enjoyed the reputation of learning and piety, and finally fixed upon John Pico, Earl of Mirandula."[11] This explanation of More's attraction to Picus has led scholars to speculate that the *Life* was written in 1504 or 1505, at the time More would have been making the decision to marry and choosing between religious and secular life. E. E. Reynolds suggests, however, that it may have been written earlier, since the book is dedicated to a nun and seems to argue for the life of the cloister rather than against it.[12] In any case, it was not published until around 1510, when More's brother-in-law, John Rastell, printed an authorized edition. The book must have been popular, for the press of Wynkyn de Worde issued a pirated edition shortly therafter.

The Life of John Picus was a New Year's gift from More to Joyeuce Leigh, a childhood friend who had become a nun in the convent of Poor Clares near London. The dedicatory letter explains that More chose the book because the life and works of Picus teach the Christian virtues of temperance, patience, and humility. In addition to a translation of John Francis's short biography, the book includes selections from the writings of Picus.

The *Life* briefly recounts the career of the wealthy and brilliant Italian humanist, emphasizing his early spirituality and learning. Picus was educated in the laws of the Church but devoted much of his early study to philosophy, science, and theology. By the time he was twenty-three, he had composed a set of 900 theses which constituted something of a compendium of the knowledge of his day, treating subjects in theology, mathematics, astrology, magic, and philosophy. Picus made plans to present his theses at Rome and dispute them with the outstanding scholars of Europe. But Pope Innocent VIII prevented the disputation and appointed a commission to study the controversial theses, some of which were declared heretical or suspect. Picus's defense, the *Apologia,* brought even greater disfavor; papal censures remained until 1493, just one year before his death.

As an introductory speech to the proposed disputation, Picus wrote his famous *Oration,* now familiar by the title "On the Dignity of Man." The *Oration,* which was not printed until after the author's death, delineates the major premises of Renaissance humanism. The first part attributes to man a unique dignity because he alone of the creatures has free will; his uniqueness makes him responsible for his own development and growth toward God through contemplation. The second part of the *Oration* explains the universal nature of truth. Picus insists that truth is accessible in some part to a diversity of philosophers and schools.[13]

John Francis uses these events to demonstrate his uncle's youthful pride and to show how worldly misfortune saved Picus from vanity and lasciviousness and turned him from the study of philosophy to the study of the scriptures. The book praises Picus for the great learning he was able to acquire without the help of teachers. More translates this section in a way that emphasizes his attitude toward the man he is studying. Where the original says Picus studied for the "love of truth," More says "for the love of God and profit of His Church."[14] Other changes in the text also suggest that More wanted to emphasize Picus's spiritual transformation and devotion rather than his academic accomplishments.[15]

Three years before his death, John Picus sold his property to his nephew for a small price so that he might live a life of relaxation and peace; after the sale, he gave all that he did not need to the poor. Here the biography emphasizes Picus's charity, holiness, and good nature in terms that call to mind the image More's own biographers have of him. This section of the book also describes Picus's refusal of all places of honor and service in words that suggest Hythlodaeus's argument against serving kings in the *Utopia.*

Near the end of his short life, Picus told his nephew that he intended soon to give everything away and devote himself to walking the world preaching Christ. Afterwards, however (here More adds the phrase "by the especial commandment of God"),[16] he changed his mind and proposed to join the Dominican order (359). But before he had time to do either, he died suddenly of a fever at the age of thirty-one. According to the Italian preacher and reformer, Savonarola, Picus's death was punishment for his hesitancy in obeying the call to religion. Even the judgmental and ascetic Savonarola, however, granted that, because of his generosity and devotion, Picus would be in heaven after a time of suffering in purgatory.

The comments in the dedicatory letter to Joyeuce Leigh considered along with the kinds of changes More makes in translating indicate that he saw in Picus a spiritual example for himself and his reader. The *Life*, as More translates it, derives from several genres of medieval devotional writing. That the book is written in the vernacular for a nun places it in a long tradition of literature composed in English for cloistered women; such instructional and devotional handbooks were very popular throughout the Middle Ages and, according to R. W. Chambers, became the means by which English prose style survived the Norman Conquest.[17] The *Life* also shows the influence of the saintly biography, a type which presents the miraculous and holy events in the life of a saint as an inspiring example to the reader. In her study of the *Life*, Margaret Esmonde says that, though More was, "on the whole, a faithful and literal translator, his omissions and additions have the cumulative effect of trimming Gianfrancesco's adulatory biography down to the concepts he had imbibed in his reading of the vernacular lives of the saints. . . . More has as his goal not a detailed account of the life and activities of an outstanding individual of the Italian Renaissance but a record of a contemporary example of virtuous living."[18] As we have seen, More alters John Francis's account in a way that emphasizes the hero's orthodoxy, spirituality, and virtue. Still, More's choice of a humanist scholar rather than a saint expands the possibilities for Renaissance biography and prefigures the moral and dramatic complexity of his *History of Richard III*, a fragmentary work which is nevertheless one of the first modern historical biographies in English. Finally, and again like *Richard*, the *Life* derives from the literary tradition of the "fall of princes," another genre which functions as an exemplum. The medieval "fall of princes" stresses the fickleness of fortune and the inevitable fall of proud, cruel, and immoral men. The *Life*, however, substantially alters the convention by allowing Picus to transcend the traditionally destructive flaws through spiritual rebirth. Clearly, More is moving toward a kind of biography different from what he found in his models.[19]

In addition to the biography, More's book includes selections from the writings of John Picus: three letters, a commentary on Psalm 15, "The Twelve Rules of Spiritual Battle," "The Twelve Weapons of

Spiritual Battle," "The Twelve Properties of a Lover," and "A Prayer of Picus Mirandula unto God." The letters follow the biography and augment its devotional and hortatory themes. The first, like the third, is a letter of comfort in suffering from Picus to John Francis. Picus consoles the younger man much as More's spokesman Anthony consoles his nephew Vincent in the *Dialogue of Comfort*. Both uncles insist that comfort is inherent in suffering because of the possibility of spiritual victory and heavenly reward. And the analysis of pleasure in the first letter calls to mind another of More's major works. Both this letter and the *Utopia* "prove" that the pleasures of a clear conscience and the hope of heaven exceed the so-called pleasures of this world—which are usually mixed with the discomforts of fatigue, confusion, and pain. More's analysis of pleasure is reminiscent of Platonic theory, especially as it appears in the *Philebus*, but it may have been Picus's letter that first interested More in "Utopian" hedonism (365).[20] The second letter, which is from Picus to his friend Andrew Corneus of Urbino, is also interesting in terms of More's later writing. In his introduction to the letter, More explains that Corneus had been urging Picus to leave his studies to go into the service of a prince. Picus's answer parallels Hythlodaeus's argument against serving princes in the *Utopia*. Picus insists that a man should never be rebuked for the pure pursuit of virtue and knowledge and reminds his friend, as Hythlodaeus does the persona More, that philosophers refuse to serve kings because they love liberty and are "content with the tranquillity of their own mind; they suffice themselves and more; they seek nothing out of themselves" (370). The third letter is another from Picus to John Francis. Again Picus comforts his nephew, who is being criticized for his virtuous life, by assuring him that suffering is spiritually beneficial. Both the letters to John Francis look toward the prison writings as they urge the reader to meditate on spiritual comforts in the midst of tribulation.

Next, More includes his quite literal translation of Picus's commentary on Psalm 15; it reinforces the instructions of the two letters to John Francis, warns against passion and pride, and demonstrates a way of meditating on the Psalms. The three letters and the commentary urge the renunciation of worldly pleasures for the benefits of heaven and emphasize the rewards of the contemplative life; More's selection of such passages out of the vast body of Picus's writing indicates a predisposition toward the spiritual life. The book also reveals the lifelong continuity of More's thought; the analysis of pleasure and the deprecation of public service predict the philosophical orientation of the *Utopia* as the contemplative tone of the selections foreshadows the asceticism of the prison writings. Furthermore, it seems likely that the fiction of uncle and nephew in the *Dialogue* derives from More's knowledge of the relationship between Picus and his nephew; the advice Anthony gives Vincent suggests Picus's counsel to John Francis.

Following the commentary on Psalm 15, More presents his version of Picus's "Twelve Rules of Spiritual Battle." He expands the rules into twenty-three rime-royal stanzas which generally remain close in thought to the original; they stress both the difficulty and the necessity of following the example of Christ. Although the purpose of this section is plainly meditative and the quality of the poetry is mediocre, More enhances his verse with alliteration, assonance, and the incantatory rhythm of the liturgy. He uses familiar metaphors of battle to describe the Christian struggle and makes physical death and deterioration symbolic of human sinfulness.

The "Twelve Rules" are followed by the "Twelve Weapons of Spiritual Battle" against temptation. Again, More expands brief phrases into stanzas of rime-royal verse. He relates Picus's affirmation of the uniqueness and dignity of man to the humanity of Christ. More's eighth stanza is based on Picus's "nature and dignity of man":

> Remember how God hath made thee reasonable
> Like unto His image and figure,
> And for thee suffered pains intolerable
> That He for angel never would endure.
> Regard, O man, thine excellent nature;
> Thou that with angel art made to be equal,
> For very shame be not the devil's thrall. (387 - 88)

The stanza on Picus's "the painful cross of Christ" recalls More's debt to the traditions of medieval mysticism:

> When thou in flame of the temptation friest
> Think on the very lamentable pain,
> Think on the piteous cross of woeful Christ,
> Think on His blood beat out at every vein,
> Think on His precious heart carved in twain,
> Think how for thy redemption all was wrought:
> Let Him not lose thee that He so dear hath bought. (388)

More moves from "The Twelve Weapons" to "The Twelve Properties Of a Lover," a platonic exercise which makes physical love a metaphor for spiritual love. He renders Picus's twelve properties into pairs of stanzas of which the first describes physical love and the second its spiritual counterpart. In "The Twelve Properties" the lover gives to the loved one as the Christian gives to God—faithfully, patiently, worshipfully.

The supplementary selections may represent More's solution to the personal conflicts raised by the biography. Despite the contrary assertions of some of More's biographers, the *Life* and the letters plainly disparage the active, political life that More chose. The biography, in fact, implies that Picus's death was punishment for his remaining outside the religious order. The "Rules" and the "Weapons" stress the difficulties and temptations that beset the conscientious Christian. But if, in fact, More was choosing between marriage and the religious life at the time, "The Twelve Properties" would seem to move the conflict toward resolution with its presentation of the relationship between spiritual and physical love. More ends the book with Picus's "Prayer unto God," which he modifies to accentuate God's mercy and generosity. The prayer is an expression of the humility and gratitude More would have experienced upon realizing that his choice was an acceptable one. The word "wife" in the last stanza of the prayer may be a reference to More's decision to marry and relinquish the possibility of a strictly contemplative life:

> Grant, I Thee pray, ...
> . . . .
> That when the journey of this deadly life
> My silly ghost hath finished, and thence
> Departen must without his fleshly wife,
> Alone into his Lordes high presence,
> He may Thee find, O well of indulgence,
> In Thy lordship not as a lord, but rather
> As a very tender loving father.

More's meditation on the life of John Picus becomes an assertion of God's merciful treatment of sinful, helpless humanity.

IV The History of Richard III

The years between 1510 and 1518 were busy ones for Thomas More, both politically and intellectually. Beginning in 1510, he was serving as under-sheriff of London; in 1515 he went to Flanders as royal ambassador; in 1517 he was ambassador to Calais, and by 1518 he had become a member of the King's Council. Nevertheless, he found time between 1513 and 1518 to write two of the master-pieces of English Renaissance humanism, the *Utopia* and the *History of Richard III*.[21] Unlike the *Utopia*, there are many textual and historical problems connected with the *Richard*: it was not published until after More's death; its authorship has been questioned; there are two versions, a Latin and an English one, both unfinished. These facts pose complicated problems for scholars of literature and history.

To begin with the problem of authorship, both internal and exter-nal evidence indicate that the book was written between 1514 and 1518 by Thomas More. The earliest authoritative text of the *Richard* in English is Rastell's 1557 edition. The introduction states that this text is from the holograph which More wrote in about 1513 and left unfinished. Rastell also acknowledges More's authorship of the Latin version by incorporating translations of parts of it into his English text. The earliest authoritative text of the Latin *Richard* did not appear until the 1565 - 66 Louvain edition of More's complete works in Latin. Although the 1557 book is the first authoritative copy in English, manuscript sources were included in Chronicle ac-counts in 1543, 1548, and 1550; the later two were acknowledged to be from More's text. There seems to be little doubt that his contem-poraries attributed the *Richard* to More.[22]

But why More wrote two versions and failed to finish either of them continues to puzzle scholars. The extant Latin and English texts are not exact copies of each other; and the Latin version ends immediately after Richard's coronation, thereby omitting important events of the English account. The Latin *Richard*, which was probably intended for an educated foreign audience, omits some details of the English book, but adds descriptions necessary to the understanding of the non-English reader. Richard S. Sylvester thinks that More wrote the two *Richards*, as he did most of his works, in segments which he later rearranged and refined. He suggests that More may have abandoned his ambitious humanistic project because some of the events of Richard's life were still too politically sensitive for literary consideration.[23]

The problem of the accuracy of More's record and interpretation of King Richard III's life continues to plague historians. More's ver-sion became so much a part of the history, legend, and drama of the sixteenth and seventeenth centuries that it is still difficult, if not im-

possible, to separate what More said from what may or may not
have happened. The known facts are fairly simple. The War of the
Roses was a civil war between the House of Lancaster (The Red
Rose) and the House of York (The White Rose), each of which felt it
had an exclusive claim to the English throne. In 1461, Yorkist
nobles rebelled against the weak Lancastrian Henry VI and won the
throne for Edward IV, who ruled until 1470, when Henry regained
the kingdom briefly, only to be deposed again by Edward. Edward
IV reigned until his death in 1483, when Yorkist rule was again
threatened by Lancastrian claimants. At this point, Edward's
brother Richard, who had been appointed Lord Protector, became
king and according to legend imprisoned Edward's two young sons
and had them killed. But the new king was unable to suppress the
Lancastrian plots that brought about the invasion of England by the
exiled Henry Tudor and, ultimately, his own death at Bosworth
Field.

More's tale projects the Tudor image of Richard III as a deformed monster who usurped the throne by maligning and murdering
his own kin. Because it was so early incorporated into the
Chronicles of English history and then became the basis for
Shakespeare's *Richard III*, More's account has been largely responsible for King Richard's historical reputation. Yet, since the beginning of the seventeenth century, historians have tried to clear
Richard of the sixteenth-century charges. And modern historians
have brought forth substantial evidence that he was an effective
ruler and a loving family man forced to the throne by the instability
of the times and by the doubtful legitimacy of his nephews.
Furthermore, there is evidence that Edward's sons did not die during Richard's reign and may in fact have been put to death by his
successor, Henry VII. Paul Murray Kendall in his biography
Richard the Third and E. F. Jacob in the *Oxford History of
England*, along with numerous other recent historians, take a
scholarly and sympathetic view of Richard III's life.[24] Jacob says:
"That there was a sound constructive side to Richard III is un-
doubted. He was very far from being the distorted villain of tradition. His early years of probation and loyalty to his brother were entirely creditable."[25]

Still, however, many twentieth-century versions of Richard's
reign reflect More's largely fictitious account. According to G. M.
Trevelyan:

Richard was no monster born; there is no clear evidence that he was more responsible for the deaths of Henry VI and Clarence [his and Edward's brother] than the rest of the Yorkist party, nor, prior to his usurpation of the throne, was his record as treacherous as that of his brother Clarence or as bloody as that of his brother Edward. But the glittering bait of the crown ensnared his soul: he murdered his two nephews under trust, and the disappearance of the Princes in the Tower, following on the violence of the usurpation, lost him the loyalty of the common people.[26]

S. T. Bindoff confirms More's rendition of the story by saying that Richard murdered his way to the throne.[27]

It is not our purpose here to determine the facts of Richard III's life so much as to see how More presented and interpreted what he heard. In order to do this we must first consider More's sources; the text makes it clear that most of his information was from oral accounts. Frequently, More uses phrases that indicate he is reporting what has been told him: "It is for trouth reported" (7), "Somme wise mene also weene" (8), "For I haue heard by credible report of such as wer secrete w^t his chamberers" (87). His chief informant must have been John Morton, who was involved in the plot against Richard, would have known well the events of More's narrative, and would have been an eyewitness to some of them. More had studied in Morton's home as a boy and continued to see him in the years before his old friend's death. It is even possible that Morton left some sort of written record which More used.[28] More himself was born under Edward IV and was seven or eight years old by the time Richard died. Many of his acquaintances would have remembered the events he describes, and the Latin version cites his own father as a source (9). Furthermore, though there were no printed histories of Richards career in 1514, a number of accounts existed in manuscript and were probably known to More. In any case, his image of the monster-king probably reflects the Tudor biases of his informants.[29]

The most important consideration here, however, is the *History of Richard III* as literature, for in it we see clearly for the first time More's genius for telling a story and creating dialogue. R. W. Chambers says that it begins modern historical writing of distinction because it moves away from the dull recording of events toward interpretation and dramatization.[30] Actually, what More creates is indeed more like drama or fiction than history.[31] The book has been seen as a milestone in the development of biography, drama, and history; it may be most accurate to call it our first historical novel. The *Richard* is a series of character studies which More creates by applying his unique dramatic and narrative talents to medieval conventions of biography and history.

The *Richard* begins with a description of Edward IV's reign. More praises Edward for his life and government, describing him as wise, just, merciful, bold, and courageous, and excusing the faults of gluttony and wantonness. He tells how in Edward's last days "thys Realm was in quyet and prosperous estate: no feare of outewarde enemyes, no warre in hande, nor none towarde, but such as no manne looked for: the people towarde the Prynce, not in a constrayned feare, but in a wyllynge and louynge obedyence: amonge them selfe, the commons in good peace" (4). More portrays Edward in terms of the good ruler of his *Epigrammata* and makes him a foil for the tyrannical Richard. Throughout the account, he effectively uses the flashback to move the narrative back in time as he does here in his description of Edward's reign.

More turns immediately from the just and beloved Edward to the villain who defies all natural and religious laws by depriving his nephews of their lives as well as their positions without "anye respecte of Godde or the worlde" (6). Richard is described as equal to his brothers in intelligence and courage, but physically he is deformed, ugly, small, and hunchbacked. In More's famous portrait he is malicious, hostile, envious, and from birth secretive, devious, and arrogant. He is also shown to be careless with the lives of other men when their deaths are to his advantage: More implicates him in the murders not only of his nephews but also of Henry VI and his own brother George, Duke of Clarence, and suggests that Richard had long been ambitious to be king. Frequently, More reminds the reader that his knowledge is secondhand, but he abandons his objectivity when it comes to the killing of the princes and says, "certayn is it that hee [Richard] contriued theyr destruccion, with the vsurpacion of the regal dignitye vppon himselfe" (9).

As More describes Richard's seizure of the crown prince and his younger brother, he further reveals his protagonist's complex and ruthless nature. First, he tells how Richard, joined by the Duke of Buckingham and Lord Hastings, captures the new king after convincing Queen Elizabeth that she should allow her son to come to London with a light guard. In his conversation with the queen, Richard shows himself to be as devious as More had said he was—with a great talent for subtle, manipulative speech. He per-

suades the queen to do his will by emphasizing the inherent in-
security of her position as the mother of two minor heirs in a divided kingdom. He suggests that if she allows the prince to come to
London heavily guarded, she will cause alarm and reaction among
her old political enemies, be responsible for the ensuing disorder,
and thereby betray her husband's last wishes. Richard succeeds with
the queen, then kidnaps the young king and arrests his guardians.

More's opinion of his protagonist is obvious when Richard comes
before his nephew and the council, bearing himself "in open sighte
so reuerentelye to the Prince, with all semblaunce of lowlinesse, that
from the great obloquy in which hee was soo late before, hee was
sodainelye fallen in soo great truste, that at the counsayle next
assembled, hee was made the onely manne chose and thoughte
moste mete, to bee protectoure of the king and hys realme, so (that
were it destenye or were it foly) the lamb was betaken to the wolfe
to kepe" (24 - 25). The newly appointed Lord Protector is impatient
to become king and knows that in order to do so he must eliminate
the possibility of a concentration of power around Edward's other
son whom the queen, in an effort to protect him, has taken into
Church sanctuary. As Richard develops his strategy, we glimpse the
impulsiveness which will enable him to become king with such
swiftness—and ultimately cause his downfall. At the council
meeting he directs a rash of accusations against the queen and commissions the Lord Cardinal, Thomas Bourchier, to get her to relinquish the younger prince; he is to make it clear that if she does not
comply peacefully, her son will be taken from her by force. The
irony of the authorial perspective is obvious as More shows the
hypocritical and consummately willful Richard asking the opinions
of the lords and politely assuring them that he will never "by gods
grace so wedde my selfe to myne own wyll, but that I shall bee
readye to chaunge it vppon youre better aduyses" (27). But Richard
knows the council is in his hands as his accomplice, the Duke of
Buckingham, skillfully refutes the clergy's objection to forcing
anyone from the protection of the church. Richard's plan works; the
queen, understanding that she has no choice, reluctantly surrenders
her son, thus giving the Lord Protector absolute control over the
two heirs to the throne. When the boy is presented to Richard, his
uncle embraces and kisses him in a scene which recalls Judas's
betrayal of Christ. More's position is again ironic; the young duke
passes into Richard's hands, and is taken "to ye kynge his brother
into the bishoppes palice at powles, & from thence through the citie

honorably into the tower, out of which after y^t day they neuer came
abrode" (42).

From here More begins to accentuate the premeditated
malevolence of Richard's motives as his boldness increases and his
mental and moral character deteriorates. Now Richard seems to enjoy his schemes for themselves and to relish playing on the fears of
Buckingham whom he has implicated so deeply in his intrigues that
it is no longer possible for the duke to withdraw his support. The
epitome of Richard's playacting comes at the council of lords who
meet to plan the prince's coronation. Richard, suspecting that Lord
Hastings and others remain loyal to the dead king's family, greets
the company politely but soon leaves to return in a rage, "al changed with a wonderful soure angrye countenaunce, knitting the
browes, frowning and froting and knawing on hys lippes, and so sat
him downe, in hys place: al the lordes much dismaied & sore
merueiling of this maner of sodain chaunge, and what thing should
him aile" (47). To set the tone for his performance Richard pauses,
then embarks on one of the most powerful and realistic rhetorical
demonstrations in the book. Here he is playing, and becoming, the
paronoid demagogue who uses imagined or fabricated insults
against himself to distract his audience from his own machinations.
When he suggests that someone is trying to destroy him, the doomed Hastings responds by saying that those involved in the plot
should be punished as traitors. Richard then accuses the queen and
Edward's former mistress, Jane Shore, of using witchcraft to cause
his arm to wither—to the amazement of the lords, who know that
he has had the deformity from birth and that the queen would
never join forces with her rival. But the scheme works, and as soon
as Hastings speaks out again, Richard declares him a traitor, sends
him to be hanged, and arrests the other members of the council.
Here we see Richard perfecting his political game but becoming increasingly egomaniacal as he crosses the fine line between calcula-
tion and obsession. From this point, Richard is doomed to play his
savage role to the death. In doing so, he has the help of
Buckingham, who is as skillful at acting parts and making speeches
as Richard himself.

Soon we see Richard's motive changing from greed to spite; now,
"as it wer for anger not for couetise" (54), he begins to persecute
Jane Shore, imprisoning her for treason and immorality and forcing
her to walk through London for a penance. Finally, the villain
becomes almost comic as the people scoff at the false charges and

laugh that Jane's sexual behavior is being taken so seriously by
Richard, who acts like "a goodly continent prince clene & fautles of
himself, sent oute of heauen into this vicious world for the amende-
ment of mens maners" (54). More's sympathetic portrait of Jane
makes Richard's malice and hypocrisy appear all the more absurd.

Richard proceeds with his plan for making himself king by
procuring the services of influential London officials including Ed-
mund Shaa, Mayor of London. Shaa, to his lasting shame, preaches
a sermon at St. Paul's Cross which introduces the people to the
possibility of Richard's becoming king by "proving" the illegitimacy of Edward's children and suggesting the illegitimacy of
Edward himself. The farce continues with Dr. Shaa's fumbling of
the line which was to summon Richard and move the people to cry,
"King Richard, King Richard." More's talent for comedy and satire
is at its best in his description of Richard and Shaa's unsuccessful
attempt to stage the appearance of the "king." This scene makes it
clear that Richard, whose plots now look like childish pranks, is un-
fit to be king. Again the people sense the truth, for they "wer so
farre fro crying king Richard, y^t thei stode as thei had bene turned
into stones, for wonder of this shamefull sermon" (68). Unfortunately, comedy quickly turns to tragedy. A few days later, the duke
delivers a long, persuasive speech to a crowd of Londoners gathered
in the guildhall. He attacks the government and morality of Edward
IV, reminds the audience of Richard's claim to the throne, and insists that Richard is the only alternative to another civil war. But the
people, who had never heard "so euill a tale so well tolde" (75),
again fail to respond and the acclamation of King Richard has to
come from his own men. The next day Buckingham and a large
group of prestigious Londoners go to the Lord Protector, requesting
that he accept the throne, which he does with a great show of surprise and reluctance. Upon assuming the duties of king, Richard
places great emphasis on the importance of the law and pardons his
enemies in an attempt to insure peace. But More, who will no
longer admit any virtue or wisdom in Richard, immediately tells
how wise men took his action for "a vanitye" and adds a damning
description of the new king: "In his returne homewarde, whom so
euer he met he saluted. For a minde that knoweth it self giltye, is in
a maner deiected to a seruile flattery" (82).

On July 6, Richard is crowned in ceremonies intended for his
nephew. The Latin version ends here, but the English text further
delineates Richard's collapse as he becomes the villain described in

the early pages of the narrative. The king's moral and mental deterioration is depicted in More's grim account of the murder of the two princes in the tower, a deed which finally brings the monster-king to the brink of madness: "Where he went abrode, his eyen whirled about, his body priuily fenced, his hand euer on his dager, his countenance and maner like one alway ready to strike againe, he toke ill rest a nightes, lay long wakyng and musing, sore weried with care & watch, rather slumbred then slept, troubled wyth fearful dremes, sodainly sometyme sterte vp, leape out of his bed & runne about the chamber, so was his restles herte continually tossed & tumbled w^t the tedious impression & stormy remembrance of his abominable dede" (87). Richard has become the victim of his own destructiveness. The "history" breaks off as More introduces the conspiracy that will end in Richard's death.

By his masterful handling of rhetoric and dramatic circumstance, Thomas More combines the traditions of medieval biography with those of classical tragedy to create a personality that history and literature have been unable to forget. Both Richard S. Sylvester and Robert E. Reiter see in More's *Richard* a reversal of the traditional tendency to eulogize historic heroes.[32] According to Reiter, More takes the conventions of the popular saint's life and reverses them in order to depict Richard as the personification of evil. In doing this, he merges form and content to make the book an "inverted pan-egyric," "a work that expresses in words the eminence of a man's bad qualities."[33] Upon this context, which depicts the protagonist as innately evil, More imposes the complex figure of the tragically powerful man who brings about his own destruction. The effect of the combination of genres is equivocal; Richard, whom More has introduced as courageous and intelligent but born malicious and ugly, changes from a shrewd strategist into a buffoon, and, finally, into a madman capable of killing his brother's children and malign-ing his own mother. Ultimately, he is destroyed not by his inherent-ly evil nature but by guilt, the strength of which implies that he might have been otherwise. The outcome is ironic as Richard turns his Olympian malice upon himself. By portraying Richard III as a deformed monster and at the same time making him responsible for his fate, More raises the complicated questions of destiny and free will; and in doing so, he places his story in the tradition that links Shakespeare with the classical drama.

But More's talent for dramatic characterization is not limited to his protagonist. There are also brilliant portraits of the Duke of

Buckingham, Lord Hastings, Queen Elizabeth, and Jane Shore. Although he is presented as more human than Richard, Buckingham turns out to be almost as ruthless and deceptive. We are told in the beginning that he is honorable and powerful, but he hates the queen and is unremittingly cruel in his opposition to her. He denounces her use of sanctuary in a speech which shows him to be calculating, shrewd, and logical. As Leonard Dean points out, one of More's most effective techniques of characterization is irony: "This is More's practice; his characters condemn themselves, and we seem to form our own judgment of them. The irony in this method springs, of course, from the disparity between the characters' apparent opinion of themselves and our opinion of them."[34] Thus, Buckingham characterizes himself as he speaks. In his portrayal of the duke, More is ambivalent as well as ironic. His description of Buckingham's collaboration with Richard elicits sympathy by suggesting that Richard has frightened the duke into cooperating with him. Immediately, however, More dilutes that opinion with a vivid depiction of Buckingham's pragmatic acceptance of his role: "And therefore to thys wicked enterprise, which he beleued coulde not bee voided, hee bent himselfe and went through: and determined, that since the comon mischief could not be amended, he wold tourne it as much as he might to hys owne commodite" (43). Subsequently, the duke enters into the game with such gusto that it becomes increasingly difficult to credit the rumor of his reluctance; he delivers his persuasive speech at the guildhall and participates with complete control in the scene in which he and the lords beg Richard to accept the crown. When Buckingham turns against Richard, More suggests that the betrayal may be explained by Richard's manner of refusing him the reward he requested: "Which so wounded his hert wt hatred & mistrust, that he neuer after could endure to loke a right on king Richard" (89). Here the duke is the loyal supporter, rebuffed and hurt, but immediately we learn that some wise observers doubted this account, knowing that two such evil dissemblers could only survive so long as they remained loyal to one another. Ultimately, More seems to attribute Buckingham's abandonment of Richard to vanity and envy and supposes that the duke pretended loyalty while planning a revolution. The English version of the *History of Richard III* ends with the promise of a conspiracy, "or rather good confederacion," between John Morton and Buckingham and leaves the complexities of the duke's character unresolved. Like Richard, Buckingham is vain, haughty, and dissembling; still we are left with the impression that if this man of great honor, power, and emotion had been better treated, he might have been better behaved.

Like Buckingham, Richard's other follower, Lord Hastings, is powerful and noble, and he despises the queen. But the narrative shows him to be both less powerful and less malicious than Buckingham. Although he hates the queen, Hastings does not realize that his actions will harm her children; this kind of personal and political naïveté is his outstanding characteristic and the cause of his downfall. Richard uses Hastings's reputation for devotion to King Edward to camouflage his own actions and then invents an excuse for executing his ally. The scene in which Richard tricks Hastings into betraying himself accentuates the Lord Chamberlain's profound impercipience; Hastings thinks he can be bold with Richard because of the love between them. More dramatizes Hastings's tragic ignorance of the ways of men and nature in the account of his refusal to heed the ill omens that precede his death. More seems to be speaking for himself when he says: "Thus ended this honorable man, a good knight and a gentle, of gret aucthorite w^t his prince, of liuing somewhat dessolate, plaine & open to his enemy, & secret to his frend: eth to begile, as he that of good hart & corage forestudied no perilles. A louing man & passing wel beloued. Very faithful, & trusty ynough, trusting to much" (52).

The *Richard* includes two vivid portraits of women.[35] Queen Elizabeth and Edward IV's former mistress, Jane Shore, are sharply delineated foils to the conniving Richard and his cohorts. With the exception of Richard himself, the queen is the most carefully drawn character in the book. More describes her as the center of political intrigue during her husband's reign, showing both her strength and her vulnerability as she is stripped of all maternal and political privileges. His talent for dramatic setting is nowhere more apparent than in the description of the queen seated "desolate and dismayed" among her possessions, preparing to move herself and her younger son to Church sanctuary because she suspects that she and her children are doomed. Although overcome with grief, the queen is too realistic to be lulled by the Archbishop of York's assurance that everything will be all right. This scene emphasizes the queen's isolation and impotence; the only strength she has left is the strength of her own will, which, although it endures, cannot save her children. We next see the queen energetically arguing with the cardinal, who is using all the tricks of rhetoric and logic, including threats, to pursuade her to surrender her son. Rhetorical skill, intelligence, and emotional control enable the queen to match the cardinal's subtleties, but her efforts are futile. The cardinal makes it clear that he intends to take the boy by force if she refuses to relinquish him. More ends the dialogue with a sympathetic portrait of the queen, standing "a good while in a great study" (40). Knowing that her son may be safer if she surrenders him than if he is forced from her, she turns him over to the cardinal in a moving scene that reveals both her maternal emotions and her political acumen. Still she retains the pride of her position, insisting that she could have kept her son had she seen fit, "whatsoeuer any man say" (41). The irony of More's perspective is obvious as the tableau ends with mother and son weeping and the young duke going to the embraces and kisses of his uncle; the queen's devotion, strength, and sagacity magnify the extent of Richard's chaotic destructiveness.

More uses his usual dramatic techniques of dialogue, rhetoric, and irony to present the queen and the other characters. In contrast, he describes Jane Shore narratively, often distancing himself from his account by reminding the reader that his knowledge of her is based on hearsay. In the description of Richard's motiveless persecution of Jane, More gives a sympathetic account of her life, explaining her sexual immorality and portraying her as generous, intelligent, and kind. In telling how Richard took her possessions and sentenced her to walk through London carrying a candle as a penance for her well-known lustfulness, More shows Jane to be so attractive and modest that the people pity her and despise Richard's malice. Ultimately, his characterization of Jane Shore, like that of the queen, is a comment on Richard. He mitigates Jane's wantonness and praises her generosity with words that mock Richard's "righteousness."

Two literary questions haunt readers of the *History of Richard III*: to what genre does it belong, and why was it never finished? Scholars have answered the questions in various ways. Two writers, R. W. Chambers and A. F. Pollard, define the issues essential to an assessment of the book. Chambers says that the *Richard* "initiates modern English historical writing" and suggests that More stopped writing it because criticism of "non-moral statecraft" was dangerous under Henry VIII. Like most readers, Chambers notices the inherently dramatic nature of the narrative.[36] In his treatment of the making of *Richard III*, Pollard describes More's sources and con-

cludes that, because of the oral nature of his information, the book
is "history" only in the loosest sense of the word. According to
Pollard, More is not so much writing history as drama; it is
"legitimate drama, but illigitimate history." He agrees with
Chambers that More probably stopped writing when he became
aware of the book's disturbing political relevance.[37] Many critics
emphasize the extent to which More uses the techniques of classical
rhetoric to develop his story, and C. S. Lewis suggests that the book
is more rhetorical than dramatic.[38] Robert E. Reiter sees More's
Richard as a type of narrative derived from medieval biography.[39]

Thus More's *Richard III* has been considered significant in the
development of modern history, biography, and drama; it is also
important as a precursor of modern narrative fiction. Here at a very
early date More experiments with sophisticated novelistic techniques, most notably the manipulation of point of view and the use of
the dramatic monologue for characterization. As an aspect of point
of view, More distances himself from the story he is telling by continually reminding the reader that his knowledge is secondhand.
But he varies this technique in a way that gives more credence to
some of his "facts" than to others. Often hearsay must stand on its
own, but at times More corroborates it with such phrases as "some
wise mene also weene" "and certayn it is." By thus validating some
but not all of what he says, he moves the reader toward an acceptance of his interpretation of historic events and figures. Also, complex narrative passages based on "some says" often begin to sound
as if they are being told by an objective third-person narrator. The
effect of this mobile perspective coupled with the long, self-
revealing monologues is a remarkable combination of credibility
and apparent objectivity. In both the *Richard* and the *Utopia*, More
experiments with the kind of diffuse point of view not fully realized
in English literature until the twentieth century produced the psy-
chological fiction of James Joyce, Virginia Woolf, and D. H.
Lawrence. More's methods suggest modern fictional techniques
which allow a writer to move freely between the mind of an om-
niscient third person narrator and the minds of his characters.

But *Richard III* is by no means "art for art's sake"; it is essentially, and again like the *Utopia*, an application of humanist ideals to
the moral problems of the sixteenth century. The Latin *Richard* is a
humanistic work written for an international audience; both versions are informed by More's knowledge of classical history and
rhetoric. It is a kind of history and a good story, but it is also a ser-

mon against tyranny and hypocrisy and a commentary on the tragedy of the human failure to understand the laws of God, man, and nature.

V Utopia

Thomas More's masterpiece, the *Utopia*,[40] was written in 1514-1516 and published at Louvain in 1516. The first edition includes introductory letters by the humanists Peter Giles, John Desmarais, and Jerome Busleyden. The book, obviously popular, was printed again in 1517, twice in 1518, and then again in 1519; the subsequent editions contain more letters praising the book and its author. The 1518 editions are illustrated by the German artists Hans and Ambrosius Holbein and contain the *Epigrammata* of More and Erasmus as well as the *Utopia*. Written in Latin for an international audience, the *Utopia* mirrors the political, cultural, and spiritual character of the Renaissance and introduces a literary genre that has continued to be popular for almost 500 years. More began modern utopian fiction with the creation of the word "utopia." Significantly, in naming the book he plays the connotations of the Greek word "eutopia" for "happy place" against "utopia," which means "nowhere." What More called "a none too witty little book" became the forerunner of a whole class of literature including Francis Bacon's *New Atlantis*, Jonathan Swift's *Gulliver's Travels*, Samuel Butler's *Erewhon*, William Morris's *News from Nowhere*, and Edward Bellamy's *Looking Backward*.

More wrote the *Utopia* during a time of heavy personal and public responsibilities. By 1514, he was serving as an under-sheriff of London, managing a large household, and developing a law practice. In May 1515, he went to Flanders as a member of a commercial embassy. After several weeks of talk, the negotiations stalled, and More took advantage of the temporary relief from official duties to make a trip to Antwerp. There he met Erasmus's scholarly friend Peter Giles and, perhaps as a result of their conversations, began to develop his ideal commonwealth.[41] In the fall, he returned to England to resolve for himself the conflict described in Book I of the *Utopia*—whether or not a responsible, virtuous man should serve the king. Using both external and internal evidence, Professor Hexter speculates that More wrote Book II and the narrative introduction to Book I in Antwerp and added the dialogue on advising kings (Book I) after he returned home to face that problem himself. Hexter also suggests that the concluding conversation between More and Hythlodaeus was added later.[42] In a letter written in 1519 to Ulrich von Hutton, Erasmus says that More wrote the second part of the *Utopia* at leisure and "dashed off" the first part when he had time.[43] Since More had a few months of enforced leisure in the Netherlands, presumably it was there that he wrote Book II, a discourse in which the fictitious traveler-philosopher Raphael Hythlodaeus describes the island of Utopia, its customs, and its government. For most of Book I Hythlodaeus and a character called Thomas More debate the problems of counseling princes. On September 3, 1516, More mailed his manuscript to Erasmus for publication; during the next year, he had committed himself fully to the service of Henry VIII.

The *Utopia* is a complex mixture of dialogue and narrative describing the ideal state, pointing to the social and political problems of sixteenth-century Europe and revealing the inherent tension between the ideals of humanism and the realities of politics. Both More and Erasmus were anxious to see the book published, and their letters show them going to great lengths to make its appearance a major event of international humanism.[44] The involvement of so many prominent European scholars in the publication of *Utopia* and the many references to the book in Erasmus's correspondence remind us that the humanist scholars of the early sixteenth century constituted a literary network very much interested in perpetuating itself. Erasmus's letters of 1516 and 1517 are full of comments encouraging—even begging—his friends to contribute letters to More's book, then to read it and share it with their friends.

The letters prefaced to the early editions give an idea of the way European humanists viewed More's book.[45] The 1516 edition is introduced by a letter from Peter Giles to More's wealthy friend Jerome Busleyden; in it Giles praises the *Utopia* for its Latin Style and social acuity. He embellishes the fiction of Raphael Hythlodaeus and his mysterious island, but at the same time mocks anyone who believes in it by telling how a series of untimely little absurdities—whisperings and coughings—caused both himself and More to miss Hythlodaeus's description of the location of the island. Giles's letter sets the tone of the book, which is pervasively complex, satirical, and ambiguous. Multiple perspectives and the intermingling of fact and fiction are typical not only of *Utopia* but of all More's best works.

Giles's letter to Busleyden is followed by a letter to Giles from John Desmarais, who compliments More and stressed the contribution *Utopia* makes to the knowledge of good government. The first edition also contains two commendatory poems, a letter from Busleyden to More, and one from More to Giles. Busleyden's letter praises extravagantly the "good and just constitution" which More has given to the world and emphasizes the moral benefits that derive from the elimination of private property. More's letter to Giles extends the fiction of Giles's participation in the events of the book and, like Giles's letter to Busleyden, jokes about the "realities" of *Utopia*. But in a more serious mood More's explanation of his delay in sending the book to Giles shows how hectic and demanding his life had become:

I am constantly engaged in legal business, either pleeding or hearing, either giving an award as arbiter or deciding a case as judge. I pay a visit of courtesy to one man and go on business to another. I devote almost the whole day in public to other men's affairs and the remainder to my own. I leave to myself, that is to learning, nothing at all. (39)

So I get for myself only the time I filch from sleep and food. Slowly, therefore, because this time is but little, yet finally, because this time *is* something, I have finished *Utopia* and sent it to you, my dear Peter, to read—and to remind me of anything that has escaped me. (41)

The 1517 *Utopia* contains a letter from the French humanist William Budé to Thomas Lupset, the Englishman responsible for that edition, and a second letter from More to Giles. Budé indicates the fictitious nature of *Utopia* and analyzes its criticism of a supposedly Christian world torn by avarice, pride, and strife. He calls the book a "pattern of the good life" but locates the nature of Utopian reform in the philosophy of the book rather than in the island's unique institutions and strange customs. According to Warren W. Wooden, "it is the principles, the spirit, of Utopia that are of primary value to Budé, not the particular social and institutional forms through which these principles are realized in the state." Wooden thinks that, taken together, all the prefatory letters demonstrate a similar attitude.[46]

The second letter from More to Giles acknowledges that some readers criticize Utopian institutions and doubt that the account is true; with tongue in cheek, More insists that he would not have made the details of his story so absurd if he had been creating fiction—which of course he was. The March 1518 edition includes a

letter from Erasmus to the printer, John Froben of Basel, praising
More and regretting that his talent had not been devoted totally to
scholarship and literature. The *Epigrammata*, which appear here for
the first time, carry a prefatory letter from the German scholar Beatus
Rhenanus.

Two generalizations can be made from the letters appended to
the *Utopia*: More's friends enjoyed the literary game of pretending
that the island of Utopia was real; and although they took his social
criticism seriously, they most often approved the satire of Book I
and the spirit of Book II rather than the specific reforms described
there. Peter R. Allen and Robbin S. Johnson think that the prefatory
letters are designed to guide the reader toward a proper reading of
the book. According to Allen, "More's philosophy is ultimately
idealistic, and the letters and verses help to make this clear"; the
writers of the prefatory material agree that the book is "essentially
about the true values which should determine society." [47] For Johnson also the letters clarify More's stance: the Utopian myth is an
ideal which "may exist but only in the mind and only temporarily"
and that ideal becomes applicable only through the mediation of
those who, like the author, "understand the demands of both ideali-
ty and reality." [48]

Utopia begins with a narrative description of the author's trip to
the Netherlands: Henry has sent More and his friend Cuthbert
Tunstall as ambassadors to Flanders; during a lull in the
negotiations, More goes to Antwerp and there meets Peter Giles.
But when Giles introduces More to Raphael Hythlodaeus, the fiction begins. Hythlodaeus, a sailor learned in Latin and Greek, has
added to his education the wisdom of experience. With the explorer
Amerigo Vespucci he has had opportunities to see the world and to
study previously unknown cultures. Although Hythlodaeus
describes many countries and governments, More tells us that he intends to relate only what Hythlodaeus had to say about the
Utopians. The rest of Book I is the digressive dialogue that Hexter
thinks More added after his return to London. [49] The persona More
and Hythlodaeus debate whether or not the conscientious man can,
with safety, serve the king. Is he in fact, as a responsible and intelligent subject, obligated to serve? Giles begins the discussion by
suggesting that Hythlodaeus put his knowledge and experience to
use in the service of a ruler, thus serving his own interests and gain-
ing advancement for his relatives and friends (55). But Hythlodaeus
says he owes nothing to his friends and relatives, has all he wants for

himself, and has no desire to give up his freedom for royal service. Persona More then suggests that Hythlodaeus has a moral obigation to influence a king for the public good. But Hythlodaeus thinks he would be useless in a king's council because of the well-known royal proclivity for war and because kings always surround themselves with flatterers who reinforce their biases and are themselves too pompous and narrow-minded to benefit from sound advice.

Hythlodaeus then embarks on a long exemplum which shows that even in England people fawn mindlessly before authority. The digression gives More an opportunity to praise his mentor, John Morton, and to introduce the kinds of economic and social problems that the Utopian system tries to solve. He has Hythlodaeus tell how once, while a guest in the home of the learned and able cardinal, he encountered a lawyer who praised English laws for effecting the hanging of many thieves. Hythlodaeus responds in a way that foreshadows his later advocacy of communism. He insists that a man's life is always too great a price to pay for the loss of mere property: "Theft alone is not a grave offense that ought to be punished with death, and no penalty that can be devised is sufficient to restrain from acts of robbery those who have no other means of getting a livelihood" (61). He attacks the predatory nature of capitalism and further establishes the background against which he will demonstrate the advantages of Utopian communism— showing how English customs prevent people from earning the honest living the lawyer recommends.

Morton returns the discussion to the punishment of thieves and asks Hythlodaeus how he would deal with theft. In answering him, Hythlodaeus demonstrates what happens when a philosopher suggests novel solutions to old problems. He recommends the methods he saw in Persia, where thieves repay their victims and then compensate the community with hard labor; they are put in chains only if they refuse to work. He concludes with a comment that emphasizes the rationality of such behavior: "The object of public anger is to destroy the vices but to save the persons and so to treat them that they necessarily become good and that, for the rest of their lives, they repair all the damage done before" (79). The response of the other diners to his recommendation is predictable. A hanger-on says that, since Hythlodaeus has provided for thieves, he will provide for the old and sick by making them monks and nuns. Although Morton passes the remark off as a joke, a friar demonstrates the foolishness of courtiers by taking it seriously and insisting that provision be made for friars as well. The hanger-on replies that they have been taken care of already in the cardinal's suggestion that vagrants be given the same treatment as thieves. In the account of his meal at Cardinal Morton's, Hythlodaeus offers a vivid, comic example of the kind of advising and discussing that goes on in the councils of the great. The digression proves another point in Hythlodaeus's argument, that advisers to kings always give the advice the ruler wants to hear, for as soon as Morton seems to agree with Hythlodaeus those who at first mocked him begin to agree also.

Although Hythlodaeus's tale has entertained persona More, it has not changed his mind, and he begins immediately to argue to the contrary, insisting that to serve the state is the duty of every good man and quoting Plato, who says that the common good will be achieved "only if either philosophers become kings or kings turn to philosophy" (87). Hythlodaeus says that Plato was right in foreseeing that until kings turn to philosophy they will never accept the advice of philosophers. More has to agree that it would be useless to advise a European king to avoid wars and put the welfare of his subjects above the increase of his revenues. But he insists there is a more realistic way to deal with rulers and goes on to describe a practical political philosophy which encourages a person to do what he can to improve society: "Whatever play is being performed, perform it as best you can, and do not upset it all simply because you think of another which has more interest. . . . You must not abandon the ship in a storm because you cannot control the winds" (99). "For it is impossible that all should be well unless all men were good, a situation which I do not expect for a great many years to come!" (101). But Hythlodaeus, who thinks this method will achieve nothing but to make those who practice it as mad as the rest of the world, returns to his primary concern—the destructiveness of private ownership. He insists that capitalism makes just rule and prosperity impossible. But the fictional More doubts the productivity of a society where there is no motivation to work and no hierarchy of power. The debate ends as Hythlodaeus begins his description of life in Utopia, his ultimate proof that the common life is the good life.

The dialogue of Book I delineates the two important characters in the *Utopia*. Hythlodaeus is by nature a radical interested in any kind of change that will improve the world and contemptuous of the conservatism of those who hold to traditional values. He is totally committed to changing an economic system that values property more than life. The persona More is responsible, moralistic, thoughtful, and sometimes reluctant to argue with the impassioned Hythlodaeus. Although we know the author eventually sided with his fictional namesake on the issue of serving kings, often the persona calls to mind the straw opponents in More's later dialogues. Persona More's comments sometimes seem to be injected simply to move Hythlodaeus's argument forward. Like More's benign opponents in the *Dialogue concerning Tyndale* and the *Dialogue of Comfort*, the persona becomes a "yes-man," or more accurately a "yes-but-man"; he will seem to agree with some very reasonable statement of Hythlodaeus's and then offer a broad objection which gives his opponent a perfect opportunity to move into yet another aspect of his argument. Just such an exchange ends Book I and sets the stage for Book II. More objects to the abolition of private property; Hythlodaeus reminds him that he knows from his experience in Utopia that the communal life is best, and More says: "If so, my dear Raphael . . . I beg and beseech you, give us a description of the island. Do not be brief" (109).

Thomas More's *Utopia* and Erasmus's *Praise of Folly*, which was written at More's home and dedicated to him, are the two satiric masterpieces produced by Renaissance humanism in England. Both books attack the folly and wickedness of the age and in doing so reflect the Christian humanist's "vocation to remake the world they lived in—to revive learning, to restore ethics, to rectify the social order and to reform the Church."[50] Stylistically, the two books demonstrate the humanists' skillful application of the rhetorical techniques of their Greek and Roman models. As dialogue, the *Utopia* instructs and entertains at such a complex level of ambiguity, satire, and paradox that it is impossible to reduce it to a single level of meaning. There are almost as many "readings" of the book as there are readers of it, and any attempt to formulate a simple and completely satisfactory interpretation is like trying to stand firm in quicksand. As C. S. Lewis has said, "as long as we take the *Utopia* for a philosophical treatise it will 'give' wherever we lean our weight."[51] In reminding us that because the book is a·dialogue we cannot be certain which of the speakers if any represent More's opinion, Lewis raises one of the questions which we must at least try to answer if we are to understand Book I and finally the whole of *Utopia*: What is the meaning of the relationship between More the author and his two main characters, Raphael Hythlodaeus and the fictional Thomas More?

Critics vary greatly in their attempts at answering this question.

When More wrote Book I, which J. H. Hexter calls the "Dialogue of Counsel," he was on the brink of making the major career choice of his life—and he had to make that choice from an unusual intellectual position:

> More's treatment of this paramount problem of counsel is uniquely determined by his unique position. In his intellectual affinities—his sense of concrete political process, his acute perception of political exigencies, and his skill at penetrating beneath the surface to the roots of political troubles—More belongs with the statesmen writers. But if his head belongs to them his heart belongs to the Christian humanists. This peculiar combination of heart and head linked with More's unusual moral sensitivity resulted in a kind of political perception unique in his own time and rare at any time. When More seriously focused that unique perception on the question of counsel the insight he achieved was sure to be something fresh and new.[52]

That "something new" is Book I of the *Utopia*. R. W. Chambers says simply that any time More speaks in a dialogue in his own name, he means what he says.[53] And Andrew D. Weiner thinks that by the end of Book I More has portrayed Hythlodaeus in such an unsympathetic way that the reader must see him as an unreliable narrator for Book II: persona More's rebuke of Hythlodaeus "takes its strength, ultimately, from our recognition that in refusing to serve on any but his own terms, Raphael is rejecting not simply what may be largely fruitless labor but what is also God's design."[54] But J. H. Hexter, like a number of other critics, thinks More's relationship to his two characters is more ambiguous than this. He sees Hythlodaeus reflecting the position More held when he was writing the dialogue: "At that time he had not convinced himself even by his own brilliant argument that the Christian humanist innovator was in duty bound to become a royal servant, that in so doing he would most nearly achieve his own highest purpose. In 1516 More still tenaciously clung to the position of the unattached intellectual of which Erasmus' career was the exemplar."[55] Hexter concludes that by the time More entered the royal service he had changed his mind and come around to the position expressed by persona More—that, as a responsible intellectual, he was obligated to try to bring about the domestic and foreign reforms suggested in Hythlodaeus's criticism of Christian governments, especially if he could see any hope of success. And Hexter thinks that More came to see that hope in the Wolsey-Henry government of 1515 and 1516.

Basing his conclusions largely on biographical evidence and on his own interpretations of Book II, Hexter suggests that Hythlodaeus speaks the opinions More held while he was writing *Utopia* but that by the time he entered the king's counsel circumstances had changed enough for him to take the kind of action suggested by his persona in the book.[56]

Although his interpretation coincides with Hexter's at some points, David Bevington[57] explains the "Dialogue of Counsel" in a different way. Like Edward L. Surtz, he thinks More's attitudes pervade the personalities of both characters.[58] He reminds us that a dialogue can be used to render "two balanced sides of a question" and suggests that the *Utopia* is a "dialogue of the mind with itself" in which Hythlodaeus and persona More represent polarities in the author's own thinking. Bevington sees More projecting his own conflicts into the characters when he makes Hythlodaeus the detached scholar and persona More the practical man. The amiable debate between them shows the discussion moving in the direction of agreement. Most importantly, they agree that royal service is inevitably dangerous and frustrating. Like Hexter, Bevington emphasizes More's decision to give strong concluding speeches to both characters. Finally: "More, in his own life, applied both courses of action to differing problems. . . . What we hear in *Utopia* is the dispassionate voice of the author, laying before the world his view of the facts and of the philosophical basis for a decision."[59]

Two other writers, W. J. Barnes[60] and Robbin S. Johnson,[61] emphasize the ironic tone of *Utopia* and agree with Bevington that it is best to interpret the "Dialogue of Counsel" in terms of the interaction between the two characters and among the characters, the author, and the reader—rather than simply to attribute More's opinions to any one character in the dialogue. According to Barnes, Hythlodaeus represents Reason and the intellectual perspective of the Ancients whereas persona More stands for the spiritual elements of revelation and divine grace. But the truth lies somewhere in between—in the exchange of ideas that takes place. And the solution More is offering to the problems of the world is that of Christian humanism—which combines the best of the two traditions. But, for Barnes, More undercuts his own conclusion with the profound irony that pervades *Utopia*; finally, human experience is so uncertain and the will of God so unknown that all human solutions remain intellectual and speculative. It is this perspective

"that puts More in the main-stream of Christian-humanist experience and literary endeavour in England during the Renaissance.
For along with his doubts and anxieties and historical confusions, he
wants to be able to continue to believe that God's hand is somehow
mysteriously working in time."[62]

Within his provocative and comprehensive analysis of the *Utopia*,
Robbin Johnson also treats the problem of "Dialogue of Counsel."
Like Weiner, he sees in Hythlodaeus the self-consumed, obsessive
idealist who has carried the freedom of the philosopher to the extreme. Persona More thinks that the generous and philosophic spirit
will contribute itself to the common good even at its own expense,
but Hythlodaeus desires the impossible—the state where service to
self and state coincide. He simply cannot comprehend what Johnson sees to be the essence of persona More's argument in Book I:
that it is possible to so order one's life as "to compensate in the
mind for the disadvantages encountered in serving a cause outside
of and greater than one's own being and happiness."[63] According to
Johnson, Hythlodaeus is willing to destroy "all that is natural to the
human personality" in order to perfect the world.[64] Thomas More
and his persona are not. They wish to reform society by validating
rather than repressing the individual. Johnson further relates these
ideas to the monologue in Book II where Hythlodaeus portrays Utopian life as a model to be copied in Christian Europe. But for More
and his fictional namesake Utopia remains a place in the mind. It is
a lesson, an idea, but not a blueprint for society.

Book II begins with a description of Utopia; it contains "fifty-
four city-states, all spacious and magnificent, identical in language,
traditions, customs, and laws" (113). Amaurotum, the capital city, is
at the center of the country. The rural districts are populated by
large farming households operated by men and women who come
in two-year shifts from the cities; thus everyone spends some time
on the farms but no one has to endure a long, hard life of farm
labor. Mature couples rule over the farms, which are organized into
groups of thirty and governed by "phylarchs." The farms furnish
food for the cities, which in turn provide them with the goods they
do not produce. The cities are all alike; there is no private
ownership of any kind and every ten years the Utopians exchange
houses by lot in order to prevent even the possibility that some will
have better homes than others—or become attached to their property. Also in the cities every group of thirty homes is governed by a
phylarch. Over each group of ten phylarchs and their households is

a tranibor or protophylarch; he is elected annually but seldom changed. Out of four candidates named by the people, the body of phylarchs chooses a governor who holds his position for life. Although the rules are strict and the rulers powerful, the government is democratic; no important action is taken by the phylarchs until it has been discussed in the districts.

Because agriculture is the common occupation, all learn it from childhood. In addition, everyone learns one craft, usually wool-working, linen-making, masonry, metal-working, or carpentry. Work is valued, and the main job of the phylarchs is to see that everyone works but that no one is overburdened. A few talented citizens are excused from the normal labors to pursue learning; they are held in great esteem, and it is from this group that the highest officials are chosen. Utopians work only six hours a day, but this is sufficient since they do not waste time producing luxuries and there are no idle classes as there are in societies where—according to Hythlodaeus—women, priests, and the rich do no productive work. Furthermore, little effort has to go into the production of the simple, uniform clothing. Although the use of spare time is said to be left to the discretion of the individual, most spend their leisure in intellectual activities. After supper there is an hour of recreation during which they listen to music and talk. Revelry and idleness are not permitted; "nowhere is there any license to waste time, nowhere any pretext to evade work—no wine shop, no alehouse, no brothel anywhere, no opportunity for corruption, no lurking hole, no secret meeting place. On the contrary, being under the eyes of all, people are bound either to be performing the usual labor or to be enjoying their leisure in a fashion not without decency" (147).

The households in Utopia, like the government, are organized in a way more conducive to harmony than to the development of individuality. At marriage the female joins her husband's family, which is governed by the oldest competent male. Women marry at eighteen, men at twenty-two. Premarital intercourse and adultery are harshly punished, for "unless persons are carefully restrained from promiscuous intercourse, few will unite in married love, in which state a whole life must be spent with one companion and all the troubles incidental to it must be patiently borne" (187). In choosing their mates the Utopians extend their pragmatic social planning to an extreme that seems comical even to Hythlodaeus; both potential spouses appear nude before the other so that neither will be surprised later by some hidden deformity or handicap. Still, the Utopian code allows for divorce under some circumstances. The senate may grant all the privileges of divorce, including remarriage, if a spouse is guilty of either adultery or "intolerable offensiveness of character" (189). The senate also considers divorce for incompatibility, but grants it rarely because the senators "know it is a very great drawback to cementing the affection between husband and wife if they have before them the easy hope of a fresh union" (191).

Like most things in Utopia, the proper size for families and cities is prescribed: when a household becomes too large, some of its members move into smaller ones; when a city becomes too large the necessary number of persons moves to other cities; if the island itself gets crowded, its citizens found Utopian colonies in fallow surrounding territory. If the territorial natives will not accept Utopian laws, they are driven out—by war if necessary. Utopians consider their methods just since they make use of land the natives were neglecting. If the population in Utopia diminishes, the colonizers return. Clearly, Utopian standards derive from an ultimate concern for the stability of the state, upon which they think the happiness of the citizens depends. Other customs also emphasize the hierarchical and uniform nature of Utopia. Although families may eat separately, it is not encouraged, and most city-dwellers take their meals in common dining halls where the women prepare and serve the food; apparently they perform these duties in addition to the work they share with the men.

The Utopians put to use the advantages afforded them by their superior economy. With surplus goods they acquire silver and gold, for which they have little use except to hire foreign mercenary soldiers; they think it makes no sense to value metals and gems out of proportion to the purposes they serve.

The Utopian educational system is characterized by an unusual devotion to scholarship. The citizens study their native language, music, dialectic, mathematics, and astrology. They are so naturally inclined to mental activities that they quickly learned Greek language and literature from Hythlodaeus and his companions, who also taught them how to print and make paper.

The Utopians are especially devoted to the study of ethics, which has led them to develop some unusual ideas. According to Hythlodaeus, they seem to lean more than they should "to the school that espouses pleasure as the object by which to define either the whole or the chief part of human happiness" (161). In fact, the Utopian attitude toward pleasure is more complex than

Hythlodaeus seems to realize; and it is the foundation upon which the whole system of philosophy and religion rests. Almost all Utopians believe that the soul is immortal and that earthly behavior is appropriately rewarded after death. Once they have accepted the full implications of these two doctrines, they are expected to seek the greatest possible pleasure in life for themselves and for others—so long as they are careful "not to let a lesser pleasure interfere with a greater nor to follow after a pleasure which would bring pain in retaliation" (163). All pleasures must be weighed against the possibility of consequent discomfort, for they do not call anything pleasure which produces or causes pain. They further modify their definition of pleasure by saying that happiness follows only from "good and decent" activities concordant with the laws of nature which are known through reason. Reason teaches them to love God, to lead a life of joy, to help other men to attain happiness, and to refrain from seeking their own pleasure at the expense of others. Ultimately, pleasure is defined by the knowledge that virtue is rewarded after death with a happiness far greater than any imaginable in this life. Thus, Utopians look forward to the greatest possible happiness in eternity and for the sake of that felicity spurn the so-called pleasures that accompany immoral or destructive deeds. In this way they distinguish between true and false pleasures. Since pain inevitably follows base pleasures, they do not count them to be pleasurable at all; they are falsely called pleasure but in fact are not. Similarly, nothing they think unnatural is considered to be truly pleasurable; such spurious pleasures include pride in possession and position and "senseless delights" like dicing and hunting. Even the genuine pleasures are arranged hierarchically with the spiritual ones ranking higher than the physical. Spiritual joy comes from learning, the contemplation of the truth, the pleasures of a good conscience, and the hope of eternal happiness. Active and passive physical pleasures follow. The active ones occur with the satisfaction of physical needs such as hunger, thirst, sexual desire, elimination, and itching, but also include pleasant sensations such as the enjoyment of music. Passive pleasure is the "calm and harmonious state of the body," or good health. Most Utopians hold health to be even more pleasurable than the satisfaction of physical desire, which is necessarily diminished by the presence of its opposite. Ultimately, the Utopian philosophy of pleasure is serious and demanding and thus in keeping with the moral nature of the community.

Clearly, the Utopians' philosophy of pleasure derives from their theology. Although varieties of religious belief are permitted, most believe in an unknown, omnipotent being whom they call "Father." Citizens are not punished for their beliefs, but they are exiled or enslaved if they cause strife by arguing them too vehemently. And if a person is so base as to deny either divine providence or the immortality of the soul, he is regarded with contempt and refused all positions of honor. The Utopians are convinced that without these beliefs no one behaves morally.

Many elements in Utopian life are puzzling to readers familiar with Thomas More's opinions; from the perspective of the author's known views, Hythlodaeus looks like an overly zealous idealist being mocked at every turn. First, there is the whole issue of private ownership, concerning which it is almost impossible to know if either the persona More or Hythlodaeus speaks altogether for the author. Other Utopian practices add to the confusion. For example, although women may become priests in Utopia, More himself opposed the acceptance of women into the Catholic priesthood. And despite More's commitment to the Catholic Church, which forbids suicide, the priests and officials of Utopia encourage those who suffer from incurable illness to end their own lives. They consider this practice to be in keeping with a philosophy of pleasure which values happiness in this life and the next. Still, they abhor suicide when it is not sanctioned by the authorities.

Although the *Utopia* idealizes a people who live by the laws of nature and reason, More had no illusions about human nature itself and constructed a society suited to the needs of sinful creatures. The necessity of controlling human willfulness pervades Utopian customs, laws, and institutions. Apparently, More did not think any kind of government could eliminate crime, slavery, or war. There is a class of slaves composed of criminals from Utopia and other countries; they are kept at hard labor and in chains. Another class is treated more leniently; they are the poor from other countries who come voluntarily to be slaves in Utopia. Despite More's antipathy for war, a long section in the *Utopia* is devoted to "military affairs." Because they are reasonable, the Utopians hate war, but they are always prepared to protect their territory, to aid friends against invaders, and to help a nation free itself from tyranny. They will fight on behalf of their capitalistic friends who have suffered financial loss at the hands of invaders because these countries and their citizens are hurt when deprived of possessions. Yet they do not enter into wars for themselves on such grounds; because of the abundance they have and the way they distribute it, the loss of goods causes neither public nor private suffering in Utopia. Thus, war becomes one of the ills of capitalism. Another criticism of the free-enterprise system appears in the description of the Zapoletans, a group of mercenaries often hired by the Utopians to fight their wars. They are portrayed as the most heinous sort of men. Their name means "sellers," and they have no respect for life and no sense of community; they will change sides at any time for money. The description of the mercenaries suggests the degree of personal degradation possible under an economic system which reduces life to its cash value.

Hythlodaeus ends his description of Utopia with a summary of his thesis, that Utopia's economic system is what makes it superior to capitalistic societies where people are constantly anxious and in need: "In Utopia all greed for money was entirely removed with the use of money. What a mass of troubles was then cut away!" (241-43). Hythlodaeus stresses the relationship between capitalism and the sin of pride which "measures prosperity not by her own advantages but by others' disadvantages" (243). In response, the persona More offers a generalized criticism of Utopian life. He thinks some of the customs and beliefs are absurd, especially with respect to money, upon which depends "all the nobility, magnificence, splendor, and majesty which are, in the estimation of the common people, the true glories and ornaments of the commonwealth" (245). But his closing comment is enigmatic: "I readily admit that there are many features in the Utopian commonwealth which it is easier for me to wish for in our countries than to have hope of seeing realized" (245 - 47).

At the end of Book II the reader must again deal with the meaning of the interaction between persona More and Hythlodaeus, for the author is still manipulating the speakers in a way that makes it impossible to know for sure whether he advocates Utopian reform or, like his conservative persona, thinks the old ways best. Hythlodaeus, expressing himself forcefully, presents a number of reforms that seem to satirize the ineffectual institutions of Christian Europe—especially those that derive from capitalism. But More's namesake has reservations. Although Chambers thinks persona More speaks for the author in Book I, he views Hythlodaeus as the authorial spokesman in the discourse of Book II. Here he sees More using Hythlodaeus to criticize a world which, despite the advantages of Christian revelation, remains inferior to one governed by reason alone. *Utopia* as a comment on contemporary tyranny and economic exploitation prescribes a return to the discipline and order of medieval monasticism. The Utopian idea is "the common life, based on religion; honour given to manual labour; intellectual and artistic culture."[65] Edward Surtz also accepts the *Utopia* as a book of reform but with the emphasis on the humanist rather than the medieval nature of More's thought. He takes Hythlodaeus's reforms seriously without imposing on More the strictures of modern communism and sees the common life in Utopia as a unique product of Christian and classical influences. For Surtz, the Utopian resolution is a compromise: More thinks the common life best when Christians possess the spirit of the early Church; but under present imperfect conditions, private ownership remains the only practical solution. Like Chambers, Surtz sees a rebuke to Christian governments in the idea of a happy state based solely on the laws of human reason.[66]

The most straightforward interpretations of *Utopia* are those like Karl Kautsky's avowedly Marxist one. Kautsky sees More, speaking through Hythlodaeus, to be a prophet of modern socialism able to make a unique response to the economic exploitation that pervaded the world in which he lived. Kautsky thinks More anticipates solutions to the problems of the modern world, especially in advocating equality of opportunity, education, and work.[67] Russell Ames also accepts Hythlodaeus's tale as More's response to contemporary social and economic problems.[68] But the most cogent writing on the subject of More's modernity is by J. H. Hexter, who says that "with appropriate reservations" the *Utopia* is modern or "on the margins of modernity." According to Hexter, it is the spirit of Utopian communism that accounts for the modernity of the book. In contrast to the traditional Christian belief that sin deprived the human race of the ability to alter its circumstances, Hythlodaeus insists that by rational action man can improve the world in which he finds himself. Unlike Kautsky, Hexter sees Utopian communism anticipating not Marxism but the radical egalitarianism of the nineteenth century with its humanitarian emphasis on improving society through the application of reason. But Hexter's argument also implies that it is Hythlodaeus not the fictional Thomas More who speaks for the author in Book II.[69]

For many readers, however, these interpretations fail to solve the problems associated with the character who bears the author's name. Two years after writing the *Utopia*, More chose to follow the persona's advice with respect to counseling kings. Furthemore, he often upheld the persona's position on private ownership.[70] As a Catholic, he could not accept the legalization of suicide and divorce, or the ordination of women. And he seems to be negating Hythlodaeus's whole scheme by giving to Utopia and its cities and rivers names that imply their nonexistence. Hythlodaeus's surname itself is from the Greek meaning "well-learned in nonsense." But nothing in *Utopia* remains unambiguous, and More complicates our response to his narrator by giving him a first name which by association with the angel Raphael suggests guidance and healing.[71] All of this hints that, although Thomas More may think the things Hythlodaeus describes are desirable, he knows they are impossible.

Since the book ends with the persona More's statement that he finds the things Hythlodaeus wants easier "to wish for than to hope for," some scholars, among them Martin Raitiere, think the Utopian discourse is based on the premise that because the fall of man has made the reasonable society impossible on earth, we can know a perfect place only in the City of God. War, private ownership, and rigid governmental controls are necessary evils in a fallen world. Raitiere's interpretation of *Utopia* makes the persona More the authorial spokesman and emphasizes the complexity of his vision.[72] Although Wayne A. Rebhorn seems to accept Hythlodaeus as More's spokesman, his reading of *Utopia* has some things in common with Raitiere's. Rebhorn finds in *Utopia* a set of images which, encompassing both human nature and the environment, show "fallen" mankind to be in constant need of control and cultivation. He says: "More's Utopia is based on a particularly unsentimental, Christian view of nature as fallen and in need of human management and labor if it is to be fertile and bear fruit."[73] Ultimately, More suggests a solution which expresses the humanist belief that man is free and capable of improving himself morally and spiritually through education.[74]

A number of recent critics, however, cast Hythlodaeus in the role of "a babbler of nonsense" and see "his" *Utopia* as profoundly ironic—even pessimistic. Johnson thinks Hythlodaeus is so committed to his own idealistic notions as to be totally detached from reality. His interpretation of the book focuses on the interaction among the author, persona More, Hythlodaeus, and the reader. For him, the book is an invitation to the reader to examine his own life and ideas in the light of the spirit of *Utopia*. More does not believe in Hythlodaeus's perfect world; he does believe that people can hope—and work—to improve the world in which they live.[75] Ward Allen shows persona More speaking for the author in his defense of private ownership. According to Allen, Hythlodaeus is not to be believed because he is one of those unimaginative zealots "likely to reduce the world to a diagram in their heads."[76] Warren W. Wooden, although he thinks More is in agreement with the Utopian criticism of European corruption, believes that at another level Hythlodaeus is the object of a satiric attack on the thinking and methods of the scholastics. Thus, "More is able to have it both ways, to agree and disagree, to laugh at and commend Hythloday's various attacks on European society and praise of Utopian institutions. The technique is a favorite among Lucianic satirists."[77] Other writers, including A. R. Heiserman,[78] Harry Berger,[79] and Arthur F. Kinney,[80] place the *Utopia* in a long tradition of rhetoric and satire which accentuates the complexity of the relationship among the author More, the persona More, and Hythlodaeus. All warn against a unilateral identification of More's ideas with Hythlodaeus's words.

But the *Utopia* is not just a book of social reform and political theory; it is a literary product of Christian humanism as well. And no study of it can afford to overlook the unique combination of Christian and classical influences that accounts in part for its significance as a work of the European literary renaissance. Like many of his contemporaries, More devoted much time and energy to studying ancient languages and literature. Clearly, the most pervasive classical influence in the *Utopia* is platonic. The characters evoke the authority of Plato several times: Giles compares Hythlodaeus to Plato; persona More says that Plato is Hythlodaeus's favorite author; and Hythlodaeus leaves the Utopians copies of most of the works of Plato. The idea for the *Utopia* and some of its institutions probably derive from the *Republic,* and the details of Utopian life are often related to Plato's *Laws* and the dialogues. But the book is not merely an exercise in Platonism. It shows the influence of other Greek philosophers, most notably the Stoics, the Epicureans, and the Cynics. And its ironic texture is probably indebted to More's study of Lucian. There is also a debt to some Latin philosophers and marked similarities to the *Germania,* by the Latin historian Tacitus. More's familiarity with the early Church fathers, especially St. Augustine, is also obvious.[81]

Finally, the *Utopia* is both an expression of the inherently eclectic nature of Renaissance Christian humanism and a "new thing." In the process of dramatizing the political dilemma of his own life, creating an ideal moral order, and commenting on the social problems of sixteenth-century Europe, More produced a masterpiece of dialogue and fiction. The *Utopia* is drama, fiction, political science, sociology, and theology. In it we see More the idealist and More the pragmatist, the conservative medieval Catholic and the modern social reformer.

<h2 style="text-align:center">VI   *The* Four Last Things</h2>

After 1517, Thomas More was increasingly important in the government of Henry VIII. But although his personal fortunes were rising, he must have begun to suspect that Hythlodaeus had been right—for the honest man, a king's court is a trap. England and her European enemies and allies seemed to think war was inevitable and, worse, desirable. The Reformation was adding to the dissension in Europe; and at home, Henry had begun his bloody efforts to secure the succession. In the same year that More became Under-Treasurer, Edward Stafford, Duke of Buckingham, the son of the duke who figures so prominently in the *History of Richard III*, was arrested and executed because Henry thought his royal lineage threatened the throne.

These were the circumstances in 1522 when More and his daughter Margaret each began writing a meditation on Ecclesiasticus 7:40: "In all thy matters remember thy last end, and thou shalt never sin." According to More's biographer Thomas Stapleton, Margaret completed the exercise to the satisfaction of her father who "affirmed most solemnly that that treatise of his daughter was in no way inferior to his own,"[82] but More's was never finished. The fragment we have was first published in 1557 in the Rastell edition.

It is tempting to view the unfinished treatise as the fragment of an exercise undertaken by More simply for the edification of his daughter and thus of little consequence to a consideration of his life or writings. In fact, it is important to an understanding of both. The *Four Last Things*[83] shows More to be fully aware not only of the transience of life and success in general, but also of the immediate danger to himself. In his analysis of the relationship between envy and death, he recounts Buckingham's fall in terms that will suggest his own:

If so were that thou knewest a great Duke, keeping so great estate and princely port in his house that thou, being a right mean man hadst in thine heart a great envy thereat, and specially at some special day in which he keepeth for the marriage of his child a great honourable court above other times; if thou being thereat, and at the sight of the royalty and honour shown him of all the country about resorting to him, while they kneel and crouch to him and at every word barehead begrace him, if thou shouldst suddenly be surely advertised, that for secret treason, lately detected to the King, he should undoubtly be taken the morrow, his court all broken up, his goods seized, his wife put out, his children disinherited, himself cast into prison, brought forth and arraigned, the matter out of question, and he should be condemned, his coat armour reversed, his gilt spurs hewn off his heels, himself hanged, drawn, and quartered, how thinkest thou, by thy faith, amid thine envy shouldst thou not suddenly change into pity? (482 - 83).

The treatise is significant for literary as well as biographical reasons; it links the stages in More's intellectual development and demonstrates the integrated quality of his thought. Chronologically, the fragment falls between the periods of humanistic and polemical writings and derives its argument from the Utopian theory of pleasure. But its most specific affinity is with the medieval devotional and mystical writing that so markedly influence the *Life of Picus* and the Tower works.

The *Four Last Things* begins with an introduction to the medicinal value of the verse from Ecclesiasticus, which shows how remembering the four last things (death, doom, pain, and joy) works to prevent the sickness of sin. More sets out to provide a consideration of each of the four things in terms of the seven deadly sins. He begins by explaining the theory of pleasure we first encountered in the letter from John Picus to his nephew and then, fully developed, in the *Utopia*. Here More applies his interpretation of pleasure to the remembrance of the last things in order to prove that the contemplation of apparently painful realities is in fact pleasurable. Again, he insists that spiritual pleasure is greater than physical and shows how ignorance and faulty training sometimes cause us to consider unnatural or painful things to be pleasurable. In both *Utopia* and the *Four Last Things*, More compares people who cannot tell pleasure from pain to pregnant women who prefer pitch and tallow to sweets (462; *Utopia*, 173). Here, the cure for our misunderstanding of the pleasure in remembering the last things lies in the practice itself, which inevitably results in the substitution of true for false values.

More begins his meditation with a description of the harsh physical realities of death, the ultimate example of which is Christ's suffering on the cross. The dying man is harassed by the members of his family, who want his goods, and by the devil, who wants his soul. Despite the bleak tone of the book, the author's penchant for drama and comedy enlivens the portrayal of the devil's methods and motivation. In his consideration of death, More uses several metaphors which he will develop years later in the prison *Dialogue of Comfort*. The description of present suffering as a medicine that prevents sin and brings happiness in the future pervades both books, and the *Dialogue* expands to its fullest the image of life as a prison in which we are incarcerated with no hope of escape and under an irrevocable sentence of death.

More sets out to show how the remembrance of each of the four things obviates each of the seven deadly sins. But he breaks off after treating only death and six of the sins: pride, envy, wrath, covetousnes, gluttony, and sloth. The treatise begins to grow tedious with the constant emphasis on the senselessness of each sin in the face of impending death.

The argument of the *Four Last Things* resembles the philosophy of pleasure that More developed in the *Utopia*, a theory heavily influenced by classical, especially platonic, thought. But in tone and structure, the work derives from the devotional writing of the middle ages and thereby predicts the direction of More's last works. There are suggestions of the morality play in the parade of the seven deadly sins, the characterization of the devil, and the abandonment of the dying man by the living. The treatise also recalls medieval guides to holy dying, which like the *Four Last Things* depict deathbed temptations and stress the aloneness of the dying man.[84] But the most profound parallels here and in the prison books are with English mystical writing. Undoubtedly, More read and valued books like Walter Hilton's *Scale of Perfection* and *Treatise on the Mixed Life*, Richard Rolle's *Form of Living*, the anonymous *Cloud of Unknowing*, and Nicholas Love's *Meditations on the Life of Christ*—which he would have found in the library of the Carthusians if not in his father's home.[85]

By the Middle Ages, Christian contemplatives had developed a three-stage progression whereby the individual sought communion with God through purgation, illumination, and contemplation. More's meditation on the seven deadly sins suggests the stage of purgation in which the soul strips itself of sin and sensuality. It is a "period of intense self-discipline, and ceaseless warfare carried on against the vices which beset the soul and tend to deprive it of the virtues."[86] Like his predecessors More insists on the incorporation of active good works into this stage: prayer, alms-deeds, pilgrimages, and fasting as well as discipline and spiritual exercise. The illuminative phase comes with the joyful recognition of the possibility of spiritual perfection. This is the pleasure inherent in the contemplation of the four last things:

For the pulling out of which weeds by the root, there is not a more meet instrument than the remembrance of the four last things, which as they shall pull out these weeds of fleshly voluptuousness, so shall they not fail to plant in their places not only wholesome virtues, but also marvellous ghostly pleasure and spiritual gladness, which in every good soul riseth of the love of God, and hope of heaven, and inward liking that the godly spirit taketh in the diligent labour of good and virtuous business. (462 - 63).

. . . A penitent beginneth to profit and grow in grace and favour of God when he feeleth a pleasure and quickness in his labour and pain taken in prayer, almsdeeds, pilgrimage, fasting, discipline, tribulation, affliction, and such other spiritual exercise. . . . Therefore let every man by the labour of his mind and help of prayer, enforce himself in all tribulation and affliction, labour, pain and travail, without spot of pride or ascribing any praise to himself, to conceive a delight and pleasure in such spiritual exercise, and thereby to rise in the love of our Lord, with an hope of heaven, contempt of the world, and longing to be with God. (464).

Illumination is traditionally associated with the contemplation of the humanity of Christ which More suggests here and uses extensively in the Tower works.

In his writings, More left a unique record of an incredibly complex mind—one that seems to have been constantly in the process of combining disparate aspects of experience. The pleasure of spiritual Illumination dominates the *Four Last Things* and indicate a connection between the paradoxical pleasure of meditating on death and the so-called hedonism of *Utopia*. Both depend on the individual's willingness to see present suffering in the light of future spiritual pleasure. And both hold contemplation and the practice of virtue to be the greatest of earthly pleasures.

VIII *Letters*

Although many of the letters More wrote between 1500 and 1520 are not extant, we have enough of his correspondence to know how varied and complex his life had become. Through them we see More as father, friend, statesman, humanist, and polemicist. The prefatory letters to More's books have already been discussed. Some of the personal ones also deserve attention. Our most intimate view of Thomas More and his family comes from letters written between 1515 and 1523 to the school in his household. They reveal the depth of More's attachment to his children and the degree of his commitment to their moral and intellectual training. More took his "school" seriously and directed it in person when he was at home and by letter when he was away. The letters emphasize the value inherent in the knowledge of language and literature and insist on the importance of education for women.[87]

Among the earliest of More's extant letters is one written in 1504 to John Colet, the famous theologian and scholar who was More's mentor and confessor. It makes plain More's enthusiasm for the companionship of the men who became the first generation of humanists in England. In it, More describes his relationships with William Lily, Thomas Linacre, and William Grocyn.[88] There are also important letters to other English humanists, including Cuthbert Tunstall and John Fisher. Both Tunstall and Fisher were More's colleagues in public service and both shared his scholarly interests. Tunstall, who was learned in theology, classical languages, mathematics, and the law, held many important offices under Henry VIII; on a number of occasions, he and More served as ambassadors together. In a letter of 1516, More expresses his gratitude to Tunstall for his praise of the *Utopia*.[89] Other letters suggest a close though formal relationship between the two men.[90] One of the letters to John Fisher, who years later was to be executed with More for refusing the Oath, is also of interest. Here More tells Fisher of his discomfort on being at court, where he sits as "precariously as an unaccustomed rider in his saddle." The letter praises the king for his courtesy, kindness, virtue, and learning but hints that More already fears the king's temperament.[91]

But his correspondence was by no means limited to his friends in England; he stayed in touch with humanists on the Continent as well. The correspondence of these years includes letters to Peter Giles. William Budé, and to Erasmus's friend Conrad Goclenius. Still, More's great link with European humanism was Erasmus himself. Although we know that many letters have been lost, a substantial correspondence between the two remains. Erasmus's first existing letter to More was written in October 1499, but the first we

have from More to Erasmus is dated February 1516. The letter is
affectionate, gossipy, and filled with More's accounts of his
attempts to get financial support for his friend In it More tells of
enjoying the company of Tunstall, Giles, and Busleiden during his
stay in the Netherlands but complains that his diplomatic duties are
expensive and keep him too long away from his family.[92] In general,
More's other letters of 1516 resemble this first one. They contain
news and questions pertaining to the lives and literary activities of
Erasmus and other European humanists and express affection for
Erasmus and continued concern for his financial affairs. They also
contain More's comments concerning the publication of *Utopia*.
Here we see how serious More was about his literary accomplishments at this time: "Some time ago I sent you my
Nowhere; I am most anxious to have it published soon and also that
it be handsomely set off with the highest of recommendations, if
possible, from several people, both intellectuals and distinguished
statesmen. . . . I am also anxious to know if you have shown it to
Tunstal, or at least described it to him, as I think you have done,
and which I do prefer."[93] In a passage from a later letter, More expresses his pleasure over the reception his book is getting and
playfully mocks his own pride, so out of place in the creator of
Utopia:

Master Tunstal recently wrote me a most friendly letter. Bless my soul, but
his frank and complimentary criticism of my commonwealth has given me
more cheer than would an Attic talent. You have no idea how thrilled I am;
I feel so expanded, and I hold my head high. For in my daydreams I have
been marked out by my Utopians to be their king forever; I can see myself
now marching along, crowned with a diadem of wheat, very striking in my
Franciscan frock, carrying a handful of wheat as my sacred scepter, throng-
ed, by a distinguished retinue of Amaurotians, and, with this huge entour-
age, giving audience to foreign ambassadors and sovereigns; wretched creatures they are, in comparison with us, as they stupidly pride themselves on
appearing in childish garb and feminine finery, laced with that despicable
gold, and ludicrous in their purple and jewels and other empty baubles.[94]

The letters of 1517 and 1518 are neither so frequent nor so cheerful.
In January 1517 More tells of being overwhelmed by his law practice, and in August he sends an unhappy letter describing the
epidemic of sweating sickness in England and the death of their
good friend Andrew Ammonio. Other letters of that year reflect
More's dissatisfaction with his law practice and his political duties.[95]

Finally, between 1516 and 1521, there is a substantial correspondence between More and Erasmus concerning More's controversy with the French humanist Germanus Brixius.[96] Erasmus
tried and eventually succeeded in reconciling his two friends.

The controversy between More and Brixius brings us to a group
of letters which predict More's success as a polemicist, although at
this time More was most often writing as one reasonable humanist
to another rather than as the pugnacious antagonist he was to
become against the Lutherans. In 1514, Erasmus's scholarly friend
Martin Dorp circulated a letter criticizing *The Praise of Folly* as
well as Erasmus's proposed edition of the New Testament. Erasmus
replied and Dorp responded with even sharper criticism. In October
1515 More wrote a defense of his friend's theological position. He
begins on a conciliatory note, praising both Erasmus and Dorp but
reprimanding the latter for attacking Erasmus publicly rather than
coming to him in private as a friend. And his attitude toward Dorp's
faulty opinions and poor taste is obvious. Much of the letter is
devoted to a long, digressive defense of humanistic scholarly
techniques for translating and interpreting the scriptures. Although
More is not so harsh here as he is later with his Lutheran opponents,
he is already developing his polemical method. He is digressive and
repetitive on important points, which he emphasizes with anecdotes
and amusing analogies; he moves subtly from apparent agreement
into real disagreement; and he is not above pointing out his opponent's personal failings.[97]

More had to defend Erasmus's theology and scholarship on other
occasions as well. There are several letters to his friend Edward
Leigh, the brother of the Joyeuce Leigh to whom he had dedicated
the *Life of John Picus*. Leigh had also criticized Erasmus's notes on
his New Testament. More tried unsuccessfully to prevent a full-
blown battle between the two humanists.[98] At about the same time,
he was defending Erasmus against "a monk," probably John Bat-
manson, another Englishman who had attacked the Erasmian New
Testament. Here More begins to show his capacity for heated
argumentation. He accuses his opponent of envy, sedition,
arrogance, and pride, making use of the *ad hominem* techniques he
was to find so handy against the Luterans. More says he knows that
on the day of judgment both the monk and Erasmus will get what
they deserve: "I feel confident too that, since all things work
together unto good, God will prefer his [Erasmus's] use of the
tongue to your silence, his silence to your prayers, his eating to your

fasting, his sleeping to your vigils, and, in a word, everything you haughtily disdain in him, God will esteem much more than all the things that fascinate you in your way of life."[99] More uses against the monk another of his polemical techniques, that of directly quoting his opponent and then damning him with his own words. Although More's letters of controversy foreshadow his development as a polemicist in English, they were written in Latin for an audience educated in the classics; thus, the arguments and examples are very different from the ones he will use in defending the Church in the vernacular.

VIII   *Summary—The Humanist Works*

Clearly, we are oversimplifying when we call any one period in More's life "humanistic" to the exclusion of others. All of his later works reveal the deep impression made by his humanistic training; indeed one of the unique characteristics of his art is the degree of interaction between diverse intellectual and rhetorical traditions. The *Utopia* and *Richard III* reflect More's political and social interests as well as his humanism, and the later dialogues apply to polemics and meditation the techniques he had learned years earlier from studying the ancients. Still, the years between 1500 and 1520 mark the peak of More's productivity in those areas most influenced by his knowledge of the classics and by his involvement with the growing community of European humanists.

In comments on More's *Utopia* made in a letter to its publisher, John Froben, Erasmus praises More's talents, lamenting that other obligations limited his friend's literary productivity:

Hitherto I have ever been exceedingly pleased with all my friend More's writings, but, on account of our very close friendship, I somewhat distrusted my own judgment. Now, however, I see that all learned men unanimously subscribe to my opinion and admire the man's superhuman genius even more warmly than I—not that they have more affection but that they have greater critical discernment. I therefore openly approve of my verdict seriously, but I shall not hestitate in future to express my sentiment publicly.

What would this wonderful, rich nature not have accomplished if his talent had been trained in Italy, if it were now totally devoted to the service of the muses, if it had ripened to its proper harvest and, as it were, its own autumnal plenty? . . . He has never left his native England except twice when serving his king on an embassy in Flanders. Not only is he married,

not only has he family cares to attend to, not only does he hold a public office and handle an overwhelming number of legal cases, but he is distracted
by so many and weighty affairs of the realm that you wonder he finds time
even to think of books.(*Utopia*, 3).

When we look at what More wrote during these years when he
was devoting his "spare" time to literature (he tells Peter Giles that
he wrote *Utopia* in the little time he could steal from sleep), we cannot help wondering with Erasmus what More's literary accomplish-
ment would have been had his education been exclusively in the
"liberal studies" rather than divided among the Church, the law,
and the classics. Here Erasmus describes the conditions that continually challenged More's literary career. With the years, it became
increasingly difficult for More to devote himself to the muses; for
the last ten years of his life the affairs of state and his massive
defense of the Catholic Church deprived him of what time he had
previously managed to filch from sleep for himself and learning. As
Erasmus implies, More's literary talent, as such, would not "ripen to
its own autumnal plenty."

Nevertheless, during these years of early manhood, More wrote a
popular book of epigrams, translated some of the dialogues of Lucian from Greek into Latin, and wrote a Latin declamation in
response to Lucian. He translated the *Life of John Picus* in a way
that demonstrates his talent for biography and began the devotional
Four Last Things, which along with the *Life* prefigures the
meditativeness of the Tower works. The *History of Richard III*,
started in the early 1500s but unfortunately unfinished and not
published until after More's death, is a milestone in the development of English history, biography, and fiction. In 1516 More published his *Utopia*, demonstrating how the fruits of classical learning
could be applied to current problems and establishing a genre that
has remained popular for over 400 years. Also, undoubtedly, it was
during this period that More developed the rhetorical and literary
skills that would enable him to produce a polemical masterpiece in
the *Dialogue concerning Tyndale* and a devotional one in the
Dialogue of Comfort against Tribulation. As it is, it is a terrible mis-
take. Under the circumstances perhaps we, like Erasmus, are greedy
to wish that More's literary life had been other than it was.

CHAPTER 3

The Polemicist

I *The Latin Polemical Works*

T HOMAS More was involved in Reformation controversy from
its inception. His defense of the Catholic Church begins early
with two works written at a time when he and his humanist
associates thought the dispute would be limited, as religious debate
had been in the past, to churchmen and educated laymen capable
of studying theology in Latin. But in 1528, Bishop Tunstall, who
had recognized the increasing strength of the reformers, commissioned More to defend the Church in the vernacular for the instruction of the general reader. Thus, More's polemical books fall
into two groups, the early ones in Latin and the later ones in
English.

A. Responsio ad Lutherum (*Answer to Luther*)
    More entered the Lutheran controversy in the early 1520s with
the publication of his *Responsio ad Lutherum* (Answer to Luther).[1]
In 1520, Luther had attacked the sacramental system of the Church
in his Latin tract *De captivitate Babylonica* (The Babylonian Cap-
tivity), which denied the sacrificial nature of all the sacraments except baptism, penance, and the eucharist. Henry VIII immediately
came to the defense of the Church with his *Assertio Septem
Sacramentorum* (Assertion of the Seven Sacraments). Luther in turn
responded with the abusive and obscene *Contra Henricum Regem
Angliae* (Against Henry King of England). The task of answering
Luther's reply then fell to Thomas More, perhaps because he
wanted it but probably because he was qualified for the job both as
a theologian and as a master of debate. Indeed, he turned out to be
well suited to the job, often matching the vulgarity as well as the
forcefulness of Luther's attack.
    The *Responsio* was first printed early in 1523 under the

pseudonym of Ferdinand Baravellus; but it was immediately
withdrawn and reissued with revisions, this time in the name of
Gulielmus Rosseus. The book introduces many of the techniques
and ideas that dominate More's voluminous controversial works in
English. It defends Henry's position in the *Assertio* and insists that
Lutheran heresies threaten the whole of social order, both religious
and secular. More attempts to set the book in a fictional framework
when he introduces it with an exchange of letters between two
friends. The letters call attention to Luther's vulgar language and
say that Rosseus (More) is answering because such a task, though
necessary, is beneath the dignity of the king. The *Responsio*,
however, soon abandons the fiction of Rosseus's character and concentrates on the direct, often tedious, rebuttal of passages from
Luther's answer to Henry.

The *Responsio* lacks the dramatic characterization and setting of
More's best English polemical writing. What dramatic force it has
comes from his continuous efforts to make Luther look stupid, immoral, and confused. More uses reason and ridicule to discount
Luther's words and supports his own position with the authority of
the Church fathers and the scriptures. He often presents Luther in a
way that makes him appear foolish and, in fact, attributes to him
things that More must have known Luther did not mean. Although
he does not develop the technique fully until later, here More
begins employing ironic characterization to undermine his opponent's arguments. One of the most vivid examples of his use of
dramatic irony to discredit Luther personally appears in the description of Luther's reaction to the king's authorship of the *Assertio*. According to More's speculation, Luther denies that the king wrote
the *Assertio* because everyone knows that he himself had help in
writing his own book—obviously it took more than one head to
engender such a "shapeless and monstrous offspring" (57). As More
describes it, when Luther received the king's book, he called
together his drinking companions to help him "stomach" it. They
decided that they need not worry about answering the book honest-
ly since their only purpose was to create trouble. But because
Luther could not do the task alone, he urged his friends "to hurry to
the place where they could hunt out the greatest possible matter of
stupid brawls and scurrilous scoffs. When each had collected a
bagful of these, he should bring it immediately to Luther, for from
them he would stuff full his own farrago of a response" (61). They
then went about to collect the filth and obscenity which they stuff-

ed "into the most foul sewer of Luther's breast" for him to vomit back up in his "utterly foolish book." So it was Luther, not Henry, who had help with his writing. By the end of the *Responsio*, More has portrayed Luther as drunken, boastful, vain, inconsistent, deceitful, and stupid and repeatedly called him an ass, a pig, and a liar.

Henry's dominant concern in the *Assertio* and More's in the *Responsio* is to define the nature of the Church. Both the king and More contrast the permanence and unity of the Catholic Church to Luther's untraditional solitary stance. They insist that Luther is wrong in claiming that the only revelation to the Church comes through the scriptures. For Catholics, the unwritten, traditional doctrines had the same weight as the scriptural ones; ultimately, the meaning of the scriptures themselves was derived from historical interpretation. In both the Baravellus and the Rosseus editions, More relies heavily on John 16:13 and Matthew 28:20 to establish the all-important premise that, because the Church is inspired by the presence of the Holy Spirit, it cannot be permanently in error; thus, its historically developed doctrines are as valid as the scriptures.

The revisions in the Rosseus edition apparently stem from a development in More's understanding of the Church, one which probably occurred during the writing of the Baravellus edition and which must have seemed important enough to More to cause him to withdraw the printed book and revise it before making it available to the public. The major change in the Rosseus version is an addition of some sixty pages in Book I, Chapter X. Here More offers systematic consideration of the nature of the Church, insisting upon the divine foundation of the Catholic Church and discussing the role of the papacy.[2] By direct refutation, ridicule, and an appeal to accepted authorities, the *Responsio* denies specific Lutheran beliefs and defends the perpetual inspiration of the Catholic Church.

B. *Letter to Bugenhagen*

More's next polemical effort is a long letter to the German humanist and reformer John Bugenhagen. It was probably written a few years after the *Responsio* but was not published until 1568.[3] Still, it gives us another example of More's early defense of the Church in Latin. The letter is an answer to Bugenhagen's *Epistola Sanctis qui sunt in Anglia* (Letter to the Pious People of England). Bugenhagen's letter, which asserts the doctrine of justification by faith and points to the fallibility and diversity of Catholic traditions, is a brief attempt to encourage Lutheranism in England and to refute charges being made against the Lutherans. It was first published in 1525 in Wittenberg and smuggled into England during that year.

We do not know why More never published his answer to Bugenhagen; the form of the letter indicates that he intended to do so. It follows More's usual design for polemical debate, quoting and then refuting the opponent's words. Although More begins the letter by insisting that he quotes Bugenhagen directly in order to present the Lutheran position fairly, his words belie the claim. For here, as in the *Responsio*, he misrepresents his opponent's views in a high-handed fashion that would have amused the sophisticated readers for whom More wrote in Latin. He twists Bugenhagen's defense of justification by faith to such an extent that Bugenhagen seems actually to advocate evil deeds. Although More insists that he opposes Bugenhagen with the utmost fairness, he often attacks him personally in order to discredit his arguments. He depicts the reformer as proud and associates him with the rumors of debauchery among the Lutherans; he accuses him of inconsistency and of distorting the scriptures. As usual, More relies heavily on the authority of tradition and history to defend the doctrines of the Church against the challenge of the Reformers.

II *The English Polemical Works*

From the beginning of the 1520s the increasing influence of Lutheranism alarmed English officials. Although Englishmen were writing in defense of the Church, and the government was attempting to suppress heretical works, German merchants continued to bring Lutheran teachings and books into London from the Continent. In 1524 and again in 1526, Cuthbert Tunstall, Bishop of London, formally warned the booksellers against importing any books containing Lutheran heresies. But by 1528, William Tyndale had published his New Testament and two books attacking the practices of the Church; all three were being disseminated in England. It was against this background that Tunstall wrote Thomas More and asked him to defend in English the teachings of the Catholic Church in order to fortify the "simple and unlearned" against the heretics.[4] During the years between March 1528, when More received Tunstall's letter, and April 1534, when he became a prisoner in the Tower of London, More wrote six books defending the Church in the vernacular.

A. *The* Dialogue concerning Tyndale

The first, and best, of More's English polemical works, the
Dialogue concerning Tyndale, was published in June 1529.[5] The
Tyndale, like More's other dramatic dialogues, the *Utopia* and
Dialogue of Comfort, is a contest between two friendly opponents
set in a carefully constructed narrative framework. Here the author
and a messenger debate the issues being raised by the Reformers.
More introduces into this dialogue the polemical issues that
dominate his English and Latin controversial writings.

He begins early in the *Tyndale* to reiterate the theological
premise on which his whole polemic is based, that the Church cannot err permanently or damnably because of Christ's promise that
he would leave His spirit to guide it. The messenger begins the
debate with an objection to the worshiping of saints and images
and to the acceptance of miracles; the Lutherans attacked these
practices, saying they were based on Church tradition rather than
on the scriptures. The author responds by insisting on the inerrancy
of the tradition. His defense of Church customs rests upon his
assurance that the presence of the Holy Spirit prevents error in the
Church. And his words echo the biblical passages that support his
argument in all the polemical works: John 14:26, John 16:13,
Matthew 18:20, and Matthew 28:20.[6] In response to the Lutheran
position that some of the things Christ said in the Bible applied only
to the disciples and not to the historical Church, the author reminds
the messenger that Christ promised both the disciples and the
Church that he would be with them and instruct them always.
More, speaking through the persona of the author, then proves to
the messenger that because the faith that abides in the Church must
be the true faith, the specific practices of the Church must be valid.
The author says to the messenger: "But ye grant, quod I, that the
church cannot err in the right faith necessary to be believed, which
is given and always kept in the Church by God. . . . Then
followeth it, quod I, that the church in that it believeth saints to be
prayed unto, relics and images to be worshipped, and pilgrimages to
be visited and sought, is not deceived nor doth not err, but that the
belief of the church is true therein" (72). If the Church cannot err
in its faith, the practices which it has traditionally taught must be
the correct ones. The author tries to end this part of the debate with
the insistence that he and the messenger have agreed that since
"God will not suffer his church to err in his right faith," the
miracles accepted by the Church must be the works of God (72).

But the messenger, after acknowledging Christ's presence in the Church, returns to the Lutheran idea that God makes his will known only through the scriptures. The author argues that the Godhead is known through the Holy Sacrament and unwritten Church tradition as well as by the scriptures. He insists that one cannot know whether his interpretations are correct if he has only his own reason to guide him. Since the Church cannot err in faith, the truth of the scripture as it is interpreted by the Church under the guidance of the Holy Spirit remains the only sure interpretation; the permanent presence of the Holy Spirit in the Church determines the validity of its actions (68 - 79). After a lengthy analysis of the correct way to study scripture, the author repeats his defense of unwritten Church tradition: although the Church may change and even err temporarily, the presence of the Holy Spirit prevents any error which could be permanently destructive to Church authority and doctrine (91 - 103).

As Book II begins, the author continues his defense, to which the messenger responds by asking how we can be sure that the inspired Church is the Catholic Church and not the community of Lutherans (129 - 31). He is answered with numerous examples of the ways in which Lutheran practices and beliefs are incompatible with the traditions of the historic Church. The author points out that heretical sects cannot constitute the Church because they are a secret elect and not the known community that transcends the failings of its members. Thus, well over a third of the *Tyndale*, a book which set out to vindicate specific customs of the Church, devotes itself instead to defending the authority which sanctions those customs. Finally, in the eighth chapter of Book II, the controversialists get around to discussing the objections to worshiping images, praying to saints, and going on pilgrimages. But even here the author's argument usually rests on Church authority. And the discussion returns directly to the central issue when, at the beginning of Book III, the messenger comes back from a trip to his university with fresh support for the preeminence of the authority of the scriptures (176 - 82). Book III continues with a long digression on the abjuration of the heretic Thomas Bilney, a discussion of Tyndale's translation of the New Testament, and a debate over the behavior and morality of the clergy (183 - 253). In Book IV, the author tells why Luther's books should not be allowed abroad and refutes some of the things he has read in the books of Luther and Tyndale (254 - 325). Clearly, More's main concern in the *Tyndale* is to defend the authority and tradition of the Catholic Church. It is upon this authority that More builds his argument for specific Church practices in all his polemical writings.

In connection with the inspiration of the Church, More defends the doctrines of purgatory and good works. The defense of purgatory pervades the book (261, 270, 301, 316, *et passim*); the author insists that, when God does not send suffering, we must take it upon ourselves voluntarily because earthly tribulation remits suffering in purgatory and brings rewards in heaven. Similarly, the *Tyndale* offers a considerable defense of the Catholic position on good works and associates it with the doctrine of purgatory: one may reduce deserved punishment through good works done on earth, preferably Church-sanctioned works like confession, penance, almsgiving, bodily affliction, and prayer. Early in the *Tyndale*, the author makes it clear that although the "ground and foundation of faith" come before good works, good works are necessary (68 - 72). In one lengthy discussion in Book IV, he points out aspects of the controversy with Luther which appear repeatedly in the later polemical works: Luther first affirmed the doctrine of purgatory and now denies it; Luther denies free will and attributes both sin and salvation altogether to the will of God; Luther says that we are justified by faith alone, without any good works (270 - 98). More sprinkles his arguments for the various kinds of good works throughout the book; he vindicates praying to saints, worshiping images, and going on pilgrimages (146 - 75) and defends the priesthood, penance, confession, fasting, and free will (131, 257 - 59, 305 - 24, *et passim*).

In the *Tyndale*, More establishes the theological basis for all his English polemical works. But it is even more important to a literary consideration of the book that here, for the first time since the *Utopia*, he is offering his readers an entertaining work of fiction. The *Tyndale* is a dialogue set in a carefully wrought narrative structure, enlivened by some of More's best fictional techniques of characterization, irony, satire, humor, and folk exampla. With the exception of the *Dialogue of Comfort*, More never again achieved this level of literary excellence.

The setting of the *Tyndale* is a simple one—a messenger has come from a friend of the author's. The friend is concerned with refuting the charges and doctrines of the Lutherans, which the messenger presents to the author for his wise interpretation. After the messenger leaves, however, the author feels dissatisfied and decides to write down the conversation for his friend. The discussion has been so long and has covered such important and intricate issues that the author thinks it imprudent to leave the matter to word of mouth. Although he says he trusts the messenger, he leaves us in some doubt when he tells us that he sends the conversation to his friend just in case "his messenger had (for any sinister favour borne toward the wrong side) purposely mangled the matter" (2). Throughout the narrative, the messenger appears to be a good-natured and innocent opponent; but readers must suspect, as the author does, that he sympathizes with the Lutherans.

Chapter I begins with a letter from the fictitious friend to the author. It conveys the friend's concern that many people are turning toward Lutheranism and being influenced by heretical writings. Although the friend implies that the messenger has Lutheran sympathies, he assures the author that he will like this bright, gregarious young man. The letter ends with an expression of faith in the author's ability to defend the Church against the ideas the messenger brings. The author's reply clarifies the history of the controversy between the Lutherans and the Catholic Church and establishes a setting for friendly debate between the author and the messenger. The exchange of letters and the messenger's arrival create a dramatic situation and introduce the characters. The friend, a concerned Catholic confident of the author's intelligence and faith, remains outside the dialogue. The author is a conscientious and respected layman, but he is not naive about the messenger's beliefs. The messenger appears to be enthusiastic and honest but infatuated with new religious ideas.

After establishing the background and characters for his drama, More carefully sets the scene: "On the morrow when he was come again somewhat before seven of the clock—for so I appointed him—taking him with me into my study, and my servants warned, that if any other should happen to desire to speak with me, certain except of whom I gave them knowledge, they should defer them till another leisure, I set him down with me, at a little table" (12). Thus, the debate begins early in the morning and continues until the two reluctantly break for dinner at noon. As Book II begins, they are walking in the garden after dinner; immediately they sit down in an arbor and attack the problems they were unable to solve before the meal. After a long discussion, More brings the reader back to his fiction by telling of the messenger's departure at the end of the day. At the beginning of Book III, we learn that two weeks have passed during which the messenger made a trip to his university. He tells how he shared some of the author's ideas with his friends, "fresh-learned men," most of whom were pleased with them. Some, however, object to Catholic actions against the heretics and their books, and one especially could not agree with the author's insistence on the importance of nonscriptual tradition. The author's response launches the next phase of the debate. As Book III ends, More's spokesman, having dealt with the problems of the scriptures, the translation of the Bible, and the treatment of heretics, suggests that they go to dinner. Afterwards, they return to the garden and begin the fourth book of the *Tyndale*, which includes a further defense of the punishment of heretics. The author brings the discussion to an end by offering the messenger some books that reinforce his position. In fact, the author has already marked the significant passages for the messenger. The books include works by the Church fathers, Luther, and Tyndale. Obviously, the messenger is to compare the conclusions of the Church with those of the Lutherans. The two break for supper and do not meet again until near dinner the next day, by which time the books have convinced the messenger that the modern clergy is no harder on heretics than were the Church fathers. The author has finally convinced him, or so he says, that the Lutherans can in no way stand up against traditional Church authorities. The book ends with another call to dinner and the departure of the messenger.

Throughout the *Tyndale*, More holds to his fiction; the book is the story of a dramatic confrontation between two people, not just an account of theological quibbling. He is always careful to keep the action within his specific framework of time and place. It begins one morning and ends in the afternoon some two weeks later. Each book depicts the characters in terms of the narrative so that by the end of Book IV, we have met two individuals. We learn that the author, for all his honesty, is not above stacking the cards in favor of himself as he does in the final scene when he shows the messenger just what he wants him to read. Also, by the time the dialogue ends, it is clear that, regardless of what his beliefs may really be, the messenger wants the author to think the two of them are in agreement. Our information about the two debaters is not, however, limited to the introductory and concluding sections. Early in Book I the author makes an ironic comment about himself that is typical of the More persona in all the dialogues. The author and the messenger are discussing whether certain things are heresies or not and the author says, "Now forsooth, . . . whosoever will say that these be no heresies, he shall not have me to dispute it, which have no cunning in such matters, but as it best becometh a layman to do in all things, lean and cleave to the common faith, and belief of Christ's church" (14). Although the author declares that, because he has no special learning, he will not dispute the matter of heresies but will merely adhere to the Church, he spends the next 300 pages both demonstrating his learning and disputing the logic and doctrines of the heretics. The ironic denial helps characterize the fictional author and perhaps points to More's own attitude toward the absurdity of polemical arguments that dispute the indisputable.

As the book progresses, the messenger develops into a kind of "straight man" for the author. He will offer a Lutheran opinion, go along with the author's logic, then make another Lutheran objection or two, and finally accept some of his opponent's conclusions. A good example of this technique occurs in the debate that begins with the controversy over the authority of the Church and miracles performed on pilgrimages (24 - 128). Often during this exhaustive discussion, the messenger appears to agree with the author when in fact he may not. He usually accepts some aspect of the author's position, then says "but," and adds another element in the Lutheran argument as he does here: "Nay, quod he, surely, though it hath done me good to hear what ye would say, yet I neither doubt, nor I suppose no good man else, but that God hath beside the comen course of nature wrought many miracles. But . . ." (44). The messenger then adds the opinion that because miracles are often reported by ignorant people, they are not believable. Although the author refutes his argument with the authority of the Church, at the end of Book I he has still not succeeded in getting the messenger to agree with him unreservedly about anything. In this way, More builds his own argument on the objections of the Lutheran spokesman.

The *Tyndale* was intended to amuse as well as to convince laymen; and that it must have done, certainly much better than the later polemical works. More enhances the narrative with irony, wit, and the realism of secular exempla and merry tales. In fact, nowhere else, with the exception of Book II of the *Dialogue of Comfort*, does More present a broader collection of tales and anecdotes. They serve a dual purpose here as in all the polemical works—to dramatize the Catholic position in the controversy and at the same time entertain the unsophisticated reader. Often as ex-

amples, More uses humorous stories to illustrate the foolishness of
the Lutherans, who slip so easily into faulty generalizations.

In addition to the techniques More had already developed for
writing fictional dialogue, the *Tyndale* introduces other devices that
pervade the subsequent polemical books. First, there is the use of
the Turk as a metaphor for the enemies of Christ. With the *Tyndale*
the figure is introduced into More's English works. It will appear in
most of the later books and culminate in the *Dialogue of Comfort*,
where the historical Turkish enemy of Christendom becomes a comprehensive metaphor for Henry VIII, the power of Lutheranism,
and finally all the earthly enemies of Christ. The figure of the Turk
becomes increasingly allegorical as More himself encounters
dangerous enemies. Usually, in the *Tyndale* it simply suggests the
opponents of Christianity; but even here it is often linked with the
heretics and other unbelievers. The *Tyndale* also makes use of the
kind of invective against the Lutherans that had already appeared
in the Latin controversy and was to increase in the English works.
Although, in tone, the *Tyndale* is more humorous and tolerant than
either the *Responsio* or the later English books, it too resorts at
times to polemical abuse and vulgarity. In several instances More
attacks the Lutherans personally and attempts to negate their
arguments by calling attention to the immorality of their lives. Most
often, however, the *Tyndale* sticks to humor and reason to entertain
and instruct its readers. The *Dialogue concerning Tyndale* in many
ways predicts the later works, establishing the major theological
themes and literary techniques, yet none of the subsequent controversial books equals the *Tyndale* in literary style and sophistica-
tion.

B. The Supplication of Souls

The book which was next to draw a polemical response from
More was *A Supplication for the Beggars*, written by Simon Fish
and published shortly before the *Tyndale*. Fish's book was
dedicated to Henry VIII, printed in Antwerp, and probably smuggled into England in 1529. In it Fish describes the state of the poor
and helpless whose condition, he says, is caused by the ravenous
greed of the clergy. He contends that the Church increases the
poverty of the "beggars" by making them pay the clergy to pray for
the souls of relatives and friends in purgatory. Not only does Fish
denounce the poverty which he says ensues from the belief in
purgatory; he also in fact doubts, and says that other wise men
doubt, the existence of such a place.

The Supplication of Souls,[7] More's answer to Fish, defends the clergy as well as the doctrine of purgatory. In response to Fish's portrayal of the earthly poverty caused by the clergy, More depicts the souls in purgatory as begging for the continuation of prayers to relieve their misery. Although he attempts to create a dramatic interest by writing the book as if it were a letter from the suffering souls, the letter itself quickly becomes discursive and polemical.

Here, as in his other controversial works, More emphasizes the authority of the Church and the inherent connection between the doctrines of purgatory and good works. Book I, however, is largely an attack on Fish and his criticism of the Catholic clergy. It is not until Book II that More, speaking through the souls, begins to advance his theological arguments for purgatory. Most people, he says, even non-Christians, are inclined either from revelation or from long-standing custom to believe that the soul lives after death;[8] reason alone proves that, if there is life after death, there is purgatory, since everyone knows that God will neither leave the sinful unpunished nor punish forever those who have been converted (97 - 98). According to More, neither reason nor authority can be found to support the beliefs of Fish, Tyndale, and Luther, who "only jest and rail and say that purgatory is a thing of the Pope's own making and that souls do nothing till doomsday but lie still and sleep" (105). Thus the *Supplication* defends purgatory and other Church doctrines on the grounds that the Lutheran denial of them defies both human reason and God's authority on earth.

In the *Supplication,* More cites I Kings 2:6, Zechariah 9:11, Luke 16:19 - 24, and the Book of the Machabees, which he says "manifestly" proves purgatory (111 - 14). His scriptural defense relies also on John 5:16. He quotes John, who says there is "some sin that is unto the death; I bid not that any man shall pray for that" (114). According to More, this passage proves that some sins are pardonable just as some are "unto the death" and that it is these pardonable sins which are paid for in purgatory and which may be diminished by earthly suffering and prayer. He applies the same kind of reasoning to Acts 2:24, where Peter says that God raised Christ from the dead, "having loosed the pains of hell." Obviously, the pains from which Christ was loosed were not the pains of those damned for eternity. Nor were they the pains of *limbo patrum,* the Limbo of the Fathers, where the souls of the just dead waited until Christ opened heaven to them; we know these souls waited in comfort, not pain. "And so appeareth it evidently that the pains of hell that were loosed were only the pains of purgatory" (117). Further scriptural support comes from the words of Christ himself. More is still depending on the application of reason and logic to the scriptures when he reminds the reader that Christ said blasphemy, the sin against the Holy Ghost, would never be forgiven. Thus, "He giveth us clear knowledge that of other sins some shall be forgiven in this world and some in the world to come" (128, Matthew 12:32). He draws the same conclusion from Matthew 12:31, where Christ says that men will be held accountable for every idle word they speak. According to More, these passages prove that payment for sins takes place in purgatory; if sins are absolved after death, it will have to be there since souls condemned to hell can never be forgiven (128 - 29). In the *Supplication*, he frequently supports his position by explicating the language of the scriptures.

In all the polemical books, More connects good works with the doctrine of purgatory—good deeds of all kinds reduce suffering after death. Furthermore, the good works of the Church such as fasting, affliction of the body, penance, and confession are especially designed and sanctioned for the purpose of diminishing that suffering. Thus, works performed on behalf of the souls in purgatory aid the person who performs them as well as the dead souls. Belief in the necessity of good works and in the doctrine of purgatory are interdependent. As usual, More's defense of good works, purgatory, and Church customs rests on the lasting authority of the Catholic Church. In arguing that the Book of Machabees is part of the Holy Scripture, More says: "For if these heretics deny for Holy Scripture any book that the Church of Christ accounteth for Holy Scripture, then deny they one of the greatest foundations of all Christian faith. . . . that the Church cannot fail surely and certainly to discern between the words of God and the words of men" (111). At one point in the *Supplication*, More joins his defense of the unified Church with the defense of the traditional interpretation of the Eucharist, an issue that will be increasingly important in the later works.

The *Supplication*, like the *Tyndale*, defends the major traditional doctrines and practices of the Catholic Church. Here, however, More builds his whole argument around a defense of the clergy and the doctrine of purgatory.

The *Supplication* and all the subsequent polemical works lack the literary character of the *Tyndale*. Nevertheless, they share certain techniques which reflect More's conception of the vernacular audience. The *Supplication* attempts to establish a limited fiction by casting the book in the form of a letter from the souls in purg..tory to "all good Christian people." More begins the letter with a pathetic plea which sounds as if it were indeed coming from people in great suffering, but soon shifts into a hard-hitting attack on Simon Fish's anticlericalism. More seldom reminds the reader that Book I is a letter from the suffering souls; emphasis is almost entirely on his rebuttal of Fish. As Book II begins, More seems to remember the letter-writers and returns momentarily to their condition in torment. But he immediately abandons them again to take up the debate concerning purgatory. The *Supplication* ends with a prayer from the souls asking the readers to leave off arguments and remember them with prayers. Still, most of the book is polemical, not fictional. Its loose structure is in sharp contrast to the meticulous intertwining of fiction and debate in the *Tyndale*. The same shift in emphasis appears in the use of anecdotes and exempla. Although there are some apt stories told to illustrate a point and a few that are called merry tales, obviously the author is now more interested in instructing than in entertaining. Some of the exempla are, however, good enough to suggest that More has not completely forgotten the value of "a merry foolish tale." At one point in Book II he employs a vivid analogy to compare the degrees of suffering in purgatory and hell to the various discomforts of seasickness. Some people are so healthy that they do not suffer any discomfort on a high sea; they are like those who come to purgatory without sin—"such as be clean and unspotted can in the fire feel no dis-ease at all." But most of the passengers are sick:

some more, some less, some longer time dis-eased, and some much sooner amended. And divers that a while had weened they should have died for pain, yet after one vomit or twain, so clean rid of their grief that they never feel displeasure of it after. . . . But then shall ye sometime see there some others whose body is so incurably corrupted that they shall walter and tolter,[9] and wring their hands and gnash the teeth, and their eyes water, their head ache, their body fret, their stomach wamble, and all their body shiver for pain, and yet shall never vomit at all: or if they vomit, yet they shall vomit still and never find ease thereof. (122 - 23)

The very ill are like sinners who suffer in hell; those who "come thence so deadly poisoned with sin that their spots be indelible and their filthiness unpurgeable, lie fretting and frying in the fire forever" (123). Christians who fall between the two extremes of suffering must "fret out the spots of their sin" in purgatory (123). Here the graphic description of the seasick passengers and the analogy between the rough sea and the place of suffering demonstrate More's talent for narrative detail and metaphor at its best. Still, the *Supplication* devotes more space to proof of its arguments and attacks on its opponents than does the earlier book—and less to entertainment and fiction.

Differences in the way More utilizes Latin in the two books also suggest a changing approach to polemical writing. Here he uses fewer Latin quotations and translates them less carefully than he did in the *Tyndale*. In the whole of the *Supplication* there are only about twenty Latin passages and many of these are short, repetitive phrases. If we consider all the Latin quotations together, we see that More fails to translate more than one-half of the Latin passages in the *Supplication* compared to the small percentage of untranslated Latin in the *Tyndale*. Still, the fact that he limits the Latin to a few generally self-explanatory passages indicates a continuing awareness of the educational limitations of his audience. These changes suggest two things—that More, whose political life was becoming increasingly complex, no longer had the time to attend to details in his polemical works and that he may have come to see his readers as even less learned than the audience he had in mind when he wrote the *Tyndale*.

An awareness of the intellectual limitations of his readers probably also accounts for More's increasing tendency to employ personal abuse against the Lutherans in an attempt to negate their ideas and entertain his audience. Beginning with the *Supplication*, More attacks his polemical opponents with a kind of bombastic rage that reaches its peak in *The Confutation of Tyndale's Answer*. An early portrayal of Simon Fish is characteristic of the kind of name-calling More is so fond of using against Martin Luther; here he describes Fish's overzealousness in presuming upon the favor of the king, to whom he had dedicated his book, and says that Fish is "as mad, not as a march hare, but as a mad dog that runneth forth and snatcheth he seeth not at whom" (41). In his most frequent metaphor for Fish, however, More plays on his opponent's name to compare him to an ocean full of evils: "For this mischievous device of his is indeed a great broad bottomless ocean sea full of evils, wherein would not fail the grievous shipwreck of the commonwealth, which God would soon forsake if the people once forsook his faith and contemned His holy sacraments, as this beggars' proctor laboreth to bring about" (69).

More's polemical use of the metaphor of the Turk appears only once in the *Supplication*. In refuting Fish's claim that the clergy makes up only one-fourth of the people but absorbs most of the wealth, More associates the Turkish enemy with the Lutheran enemy (44). As in the *Tyndale,* he insists that the heathen enemies of Christianity can succeed only if they are aided by the destructive power of the Lutherans.

As literature the *Supplication* cannot compare with More's dialogues; its use of irony, satire, characterization, and dramatic exempla is limited. In deference to the expectations of his audience, he restricts his use of Latin and increasingly turns from witty tales to scurrilous attacks on the Lutherans in order to entertain and persuade. The need to influence the vernacular reader was becoming urgent as the power of the Lutherans mounted; and undoubtedly, More as a member of the king's council and then Chancellor no longer had time to make his polemics polished works of fiction.

C.   *The* Confutation of Tyndale's Answer

Thomas More's third polemical work in English was occasioned by William Tyndale's *Answer unto Sir Thomas More's Dialogue,* published in the spring of 1531. Tyndale's main concerns in the *Answer* are to refute More's defense of the lasting authority and unwritten traditions of the Church and to discredit pilgrimages, the worship of the Blessed Sacrament, and the worship of images and relics. Although More had defended Church authority and practices extensively in the *Dialogue concerning Tyndale,* he felt compelled to respond to Tyndale's new attack and in 1532 published the first three books of his *Confutation of Tyndale's Answer.* The remaining five books appeared in 1533.[10]

The *Confutation,* like all the polemical books, builds its argument on the premise that the Church, instituted by God and informed by the Holy Ghost, "hath ever the true judgment." More bases his position on the written and unwritten tradition of the Church and reminds the reader of it constantly. He assumes the correctness of the traditions of the Church and the opinions of the Church fathers, insisting that everything contrary to the divinely established and guided Church is in error and everything that is a part of it carries the assurance of inspiration. In this context, he defends specific Church customs and doctrines.

More sets the tone of the book early, using irony to establish his opinion of Tyndale, whom he accuses of believing in neither the doctrine of good works nor the kinds of works recommended by the Church. He justifies and interprets the practice of alms-giving, penance, prayers, fasting, confession, and the worshiping of saints and relics, all of which protect Christians from sin in this world and help remit suffering in purgatory. He accuses the Lutherans of saying that the Holy Sacrament is nothing "but bare brede" and presents in detail the traditional Catholic interpretation of the Eucharist.

Although More's theological position is essentially the same in all the polemical books, technically there are marked differences between the *Confutation* and the two preceding works. The *Confutation* makes no attempt to present the polemic in the form of a narrative, but merely sets out quotations from the opponents' writing and refutes them. Yet, More remains aware of his readers; he includes some dramatic tales and increasingly plays to his audience with attacks on the character and morality of his opponents. His scurrility has clearly become a deliberate effort not just to undermine the opinions of the Lutherans but also to amuse his readers. To effect his dual purpose, he often uses the preacher's time-honored methods of dramatizing his position with humorous, abusive, and sometimes bawdy exempla. He frequently mocks his opponents by twisting their ideas so that they appear to advocate the very things they argue against. Obviously, More means to entertain his audience as well as to instruct them with his depiction of the immoral Lutherans who so foolishly get entangled in their own arguments. Indeed, More never misses an opportunity to disparage Lutheran beliefs by attacking the morality of the men who espouse them. He knew that at least some of his audience were more likely to respond to the derision of their enemies then to uninterrupted theological discourse. Still, the *Confutation* contains long polemical and theological discussions such as never appear in the more narrative and concise *Tyndale*. The seemingly endless analysis of Tyndale's translation of the scriptures which dominates more than 200 pages of Book III would have appeared excessive to any audience More might have had in mind, certainly to the unlearned laymen for whom he wrote.

We have already seen More employing far less Latin in the *Supplication* than he did in the *Tyndale* and being less careful in the translation of it. The *Confutation* continues the trend. Here again Latin occurs less frequently, and well over one-half the phrases and sentences remain untranslated and receive little explanation. Frequently, More neglects to translate even those Latin passages that are important to an understanding of the English. Although he reveals his concern for his audience in other ways, he obviously now has even less time to devote to the literary details of his presentation than he did in writing the *Supplication*.

The presence of the dramatic exemplum and the humorous characterization of the Lutherans indicates More's continuing desire to interest his readers. In fact, the *Confutation* comments directly on its audience, revealing More's image of the people for whom he writes. He refers frequently to his and Tyndale's audience in words that echo Bishop Tunstall's letter instructing him to defend the Church in the vernacular in order to fortify "simple and unlearned" people against the temptation to heresy. In a fictional account of a conversation between two English women and the Lutheran polemicist Robert Barnes, More dramatizes his idea of the English vernacular audience. A merchant's wife comes to Barnes because reading his books in English has confused her. Representing the naive vernacular reader, she insists that she needs a known, informed tradition. Finally, she outtalks the talkative Barnes on the subject of the true nature of the Church. Next, Barnes's bawdy, illiterate hostess, the Wife of the Bottle of Botolph's Wharf, challenges his circular arguments and attacks his "secret, unknown, spiritual" Church. The vignette ends with a long rhetorical speech in which the merchant's wife compares the nurturing Catholic Church to the new church which offers neither guidance nor comfort—just confusion. Thus Barnes is humiliated by two women, one who can only read English and one who cannot read at all. In the tale of the women and Friar Barnes, More points to the limitations and strengths of his readers (883 - 906). Although they are theologically unsophisticated, they understand the Church and with the proper guidance can defend themselves against the sophistical arguments of the heretics. But they need and want the kind of direction the traditional Church offers—most of them cannot interpret the scriptures; some cannot even read them. More's Church is still present to do the things the new church would leave to the unlettered layman. As usual, More's defense of the Church rests on his faith in the validity of unwritten, as well as the written, tradition.

D.   The Reply to John Frith *and* The Apology of Sir Thomas More, Knight

In 1532, while More was writing the *Confutation*, a young

Lutheran, John Frith, was being held in the Tower for heresy. During his imprisonment, Frith wrote his opinions concerning the doctrine of the real presence of the body and blood of Christ in the Sacrament. More got a copy of Frith's treatise and composed a reply, which he published in 1533 as a letter to a friend.[11] More's *Reply* refutes Frith's assertion that transubstantiation is impossible and defends the Catholic interpretation of the Eucharist. In contrast to the previous works, More makes no attempt to enliven the letter with drama, narrative, or humor. He relies heavily on argumentation and on the authority of the Church fathers and the scriptures to deny Frith's claim that scriptural descriptions of the Sacrament must be allegorical since it is impossible for Christ's body to be in two places at once. The *Reply* is a brief defense of one important element in the Catholic tradition and was probably intended for a smaller and more intellectual audience than were the other polemical works.

Near the end of the letter we glimpse More's discouragement over the controversy between Catholics and Reformers. He was beginning to be concerned about the quality of his books, which he knew were too long. Here he says: "Lo in stede of a letter haue you almost a boke, longer than I truste good Chrysten folke shall nede in so clere an artycle of the fayth, and to all fast faythfull peple so farre out of all dowt, sauynge that in sendying you your copy agayne, me thoughte I muste nedes wryte you somwhat what I my selfe thoughte of his [Frith's] wrytyng."[12] Although More suspects that the faithful do not need his books and that the faithless are not changed by them, he is tempted to make the letter even longer by writing about other issues. The Reformers were raising questions faster than More could answer them—and he was running out of time.

Thomas More finished his *Reply to Frith* in December 1532. In March of that year, the House of Commons had drawn up a list of complaints against the clergy as part of the attempt to coerce them into siding with Henry on the divorce. The Complaint stated that discord between the king's "spiritual and temporal" subjects was threatening the peace of the country. Later that year a lawyer, Christopher Saint-German, published his anonymous *Treatise concerning the Division between the Spiritualty and Temporalty*. The *Division* is similar in spirit to the Complaint and, like it, suggests that the disagreements between clergy and laity were of recent origin. It was in response to Saint-German's treatise that More wrote *The Apology of Sir Thomas More, Knight.*[13] In the *Division*, Saint-German, who claims to be a loyal Catholic, discusses the causes of discord and says that the purpose of his book is to reconcile the laity and the clergy. It is clear, however, that he blames the clergy. His list of accusations against them includes not only real faults but rumored and fabricated ones as well.

The *Apology* defends the clergy against Saint-German's accusations of greed, pride, laziness, and the cruel, irresponsible treatment of heretics. Frequently, More rebukes Saint-German for his sweeping generalizations, but he admits that some members of the clergy abuse their positions just as some laymen do (70 - 79); he himself reprimands the clergy for their offenses but defends them against most of Saint-German's accusations. In addition to defending the clergy, in the *Apology* More reasserts other issues characteristic of his polemical stance. He insists on the authority and inspiration of Church traditions and emphasizes the weakness of Lutheran attempts to discredit them (14 - 35, 112 - 14, 191 - 94); he justifies the Church position on faith, good works, and purgatory (38, 113 - 14). Thus, the theological assumptions of the *Apology* parallel those of the other polemical works; it differs from them only in the extent to which More defends the clergy.

The *Apology* further demonstrates More's uneasiness over the quality of his controversial writing. Here he responds to critics who say his books are too long by insisting that their repetitiveness is a result of his desire to avoid misrepresenting the opinions of his opponents as they misrepresent his. He says that his lengthy arguments are necessary because his subject is important and because a heresy can be written in a moment while a reasonable and valid answer, which must be carefully composed, takes much longer. He adds that his books, especially the *Confutation*, tend to be long and repetitious because he wants each chapter to be a complete and convincing answer to all the heresies of Tyndale and Barnes (1 - 10). More's justification suggests that he was writing to an audience more inclined to read a chapter than a whole book and more easily moved to heresy than against it.

More comments directly on two other aspects of his polemical style: the use of the vernacular and of the dramatic exempla. In reprimanding Saint-German for his irresponsible criticism of the clergy, More implies that nothing should be written in English that is not suited to the limitations of the lay person and compares Saint-German to John Gerson, who circumspectly criticized the clergy in

Latin (66). From the same perspective on his audience, he defends
the use of "fansyes and sportes, and mery tales" in serious writing
by quoting Horace, who says that a man may sometimes tell the
truth in sport (194). He also deals with the problem in the introduction to the *Tyndale*, where he tells how, before publishing that
book, he submitted it to men "better learned" than himself to
ascertain their opinions of his fictional Lutheran sympathizer and of
his "tales and merry words." He shows that there are precedents for
the kind of exempla he uses in the works of earlier polemicists and
of the saints. Still, he assures us that he included in the published
book only those things that most of his advisors approved (*Tyndale*,
3). Similarly in the *Confutation*, he introduces the elaborate tale of
Friar Barnes and the two women with a justification of fiction as a
teaching device: "But now good chrysten readers, to the entent that
the foly of frere Barons inuencyon may the more clerely appere con-
cernyng his tokens with whiche he techeth vs to know his vnknowen
chyrch / let vs yet a lytell consyder hys lesson better. Let vs suppose. . . ." (*Confutation*, 883), and he begins the tale. He was concerned that his satire and fiction be read for what it was, a technique for illustrating the lessons he wanted his readers to learn. In
fact, however, the *Apology* contains little fiction; most of the book
is devoted to arguing against the quotations More selects from the
Division. But it is replete with examples of his attempts to entertain
his audience by satirizing his opponents (8, 9, 31 - 32, 43 - 51, 82).
Frequently, in both the *Confutation* and the *Apology*, More turns
the argument to his advantage by abandoning the issues to attack
the Lutherans, who he says are guilty of much worse offenses than
those they abhor in Catholicism. Thus, the *Apology* extends More's
tendency to replace the dramatic, "merry" tale of the earlier books
with vitriolic, if sometimes humorous, satire. There is also a continuation of the trend toward a limited use of Latin. Only eleven
different Latin phrases occur in More's text; of these only two are
translated or explained in any detail (14 - 30). Although More was
not attending as assiduously to the literary aspects of his later
polemics as he had in earlier work, he was developing some definite
theories about polemical writing in the vernacular.

E.   The Debellation of Salem and Bizance

In 1533 Saint-German answered More's *Apology* with his
Dialogue betwixt Salem and Bizance. Immediately, More responded with *The Debellation of Salem and Bizance* [14] The title of

the book suggests More's attitude toward his conflict with the Reformers; the *Oxford English Dictionary* defines "debellation" as "the action of vanquishing or reducing by force of arms; conquest, subjugation." More begins the book with an excuse for repeating the defense of the clergy, canon law, and the *ex officio* summoning of heretics, already presented in the *Apology*. He explains that he undertakes to refute Saint-German again only because he fears the new book will intimidate the clergy into neglecting their duty to prosecute heretics and thereby "decay the fayth."

The polemical content of the *Debellation* is more limited than that of the preceding works. Most of the book is devoted to a legalistic reexamination of Saint-German's attacks on the clergy and canon law, with little attention to the doctrines concerning faith, good works, and purgatory. But as usual, More expresses his basic, now almost obsessive, concern for the survival of the traditional Church. This is the polemical issue that pervades the book's quibbling repetitiveness. Early in the *Debellation,* More says that the real purpose of the *Apology* had been to defend "the very good old and long approued lawes, both of thys realme and of the whole corps of christendome" (932). Throughout the *Debellation,* he reminds the reader that his defense of the clergy is actually a defense of the Roman Church, which for More was "the whole corps of christendome." And as the book ends, there can be no doubt that the point, in what at times seems like a pointless discourse, is the most important issue in his polemic; the defense of the clergy becomes a defense of the authority of the Church (1033 - 34).

Throughout the *Debellation,* More chastises Saint-German for criticizing the clergy in English and reiterates his opinion that, given the nature of the vernacular audience, one should not deal with controversial matters in English. He insists that his opponent's only motive for using English is to exploit the hostility of the laity toward the clergy (937). Later, he shows the extent to which he believes the common audience should be protected from religious argument by saying that he no more approves the free discussion of heresy than the free discussion of treason. He thinks that to inform the people about heresy will tempt them to it just as it would tempt them to sin if one were to describe all the degrees and ways of sinning (964 - 65). More's image of the audience for which he writes becomes increasingly clear in the final books.

More shows an inclination to return to careful translation of significant Latin passages in the *Debellation* despite some long and confusing references to Church law; most of the important Latin quotations are translated (948, 952, 953, 964, 966, 980, 1032). And again he is employing a variety of techniques to entertain his readers—anecdotes, folk analogies, and sarcasm; he indicates the importance he attaches to the fictional aspects of polemics by criticizing the absence of literary focus in Saint-German's *Salem and Bizance.* He mocks his opponent's rhetorical ineffectiveness and accuses him of carelessly creating unbelievable characters and situations. At times in the *Debellation,* More is at his satirical best as he combines humor and irony to expose his opponent's foolishness. Without resorting to the malicious personal attacks of the *Supplication,* the *Confutation,* and the *Apology,* he implies that Saint-German is insincere and his theology unacceptable. Occasionally, he derides both himself and his opponent for their wearisome haggling. Although More enlivens the otherwise dreary legal debate with exempla and humor, he generally avoids the degree of scurrility that dominates the preceding books. The criticism in the *Debellation* is almost always directed against Saint-German's argument rather than against him; and even when the attack is personal, it is much less abusive than that of the other books. More may imply that his opponent is a liar and a fool but never an adulterer or a murderer, and seldom a heretic.

The figure of the Turk, which was absent in the *Apology,* turns up again as a polemical device in the *Debellation,* first in "The declaracion of the tytle" in which More explains that Salem and Bizance were once two towns under the "great Turke" (929). Here the reference is to the Turk as a historical figure. But near the end of the book there is a suggestion of the figurative link between the Turk and the Lutherans (1030).

With the exception of its fundamental defense of the authority of the Catholic Church, the *Debellation* has little connection with the important issues of the other controversial works. Although critics have generally considered it and the *Answer to the Poisoned Book* to be inferior to the earlier books,[15] here, in a brief return to some of the literary techniques of the *Tyndale,* More reminds us that he is still capable of the skillful combination of fiction, drama, and instruction which he will demonstrate for the last time in the prison *Dialogue of Comfort.*

F. *The* Answer to the Poisoned Book

More completed the last of his polemical works, the *Answer to the Poisoned Book,*[16] late in 1533, only a few months before his imprisonment.[17] The book attacks the opinions of an anonymous work called *The Supper of the Lord,* the author of which is usually considered to be William Tyndale although some scholars still think it may have been written by another Reformer, George Joye.[18] It is difficult to defend the *Answer* against scholars who see significant literary deterioration in More's last two controversial books. The *Answer* is a digressive and often repetitive defense of the doctrine of the real presence. Early in the *Answer,* More takes the Catholic position that the bread and wine of the Eucharist become the body and blood of Chirst. He continually returns to this point, employing the words of Christ and the writings of the Church for support. Yet Louis L. Martz says that the *Answer,* with its passionate defense of the real presence, contains "the center of More's spiritual life" and reveals the "essential aim" of his polemics—to prevent "a breach between flesh and spirit."[19]

The *Answer,* like the *Debellation,* is linked to the earlier controversial works by its emphasis on Church tradition and authority. More insists throughout that his position is the historical one of the Church, the whole body of Christendom, and the scriptures. Here, however, he is not defending the authority of the Church so much as using that authority to buttress his arguments concerning the Eucharist. The *Answer* asserts both the necessity for good works and the preeminence of faith. Occasionally, it treats in the usual manner other issues of importance in the earlier works—pilgrimages, the worshiping of saints and images, and the traditional services of the Church. In general, the polemical emphasis in the *Answer* is on Church tradition, the Eucharist, and the necessity of good works.

In the *Answer,* which contains almost no exempla, More reverts to his calumnious attacks on the Lutherans, though seldom with the stridency of the *Supplication,* the *Confutation,* and the *Apology.* Perhaps his treatment of his enemies in the *Answer* represents an attempt to amuse, but it is a poor offering compared to the tales and debates of the early books. Finally, there appears in the *Answer* a kind of macabre imagery which is, with the exception of the *Four Last Things,* uncharacteristic of More's writing. Throughout the *Answer,* More describes in gruesome detail the Jews' and Saint-German's misunderstanding of Christ's description of the Eucharist. This passage is typical:

For the Jewes had an opinion that he would haue them eat hys fleshe in the very forme of fleshe, and (as saynte Austine sayth) they thoughte they should eate it deade cut oute in gobbettes as shepes fleshe is in the shamels. . . . Doth any man that receyueth the blessed sacrament, thinke (as the Jewes thought) that the flesh of Christe that he receiueth, is in the forme of fleshe, cutte out in gobbettes as sheepes fleshe is solde in the shamels and not in the forme of breade? (1085).

More uses an equally unpleasant analogy to describe the Lutheran position on faith and works. He tells how people so objected to the heretical doctrine of "faith alone" that the Lutherans needed "some plasters of false gloses, to heale the foule marmole[20] of theyr scabbed shynnes, that they had gotten by that text of theyr false faythe alone" (1088). More goes on to tell how the Lutherans then tried to plaster the sore by modifying their definition of faith to include hope and charity (1089). The use of ugly physical images are probably more a reflection of the writer's state of mind than an attempt to find something new to appeal to the "simple" reader.

The *Answer* does, at least, show some concern for the audience in the translation of important Latin quotations. Here, as in the *Debellation*, More is more careful to translate than he is in the immediately preceding works. Of the complete Latin sentences in the book, all are translated and some of these are carefully explicated to clarify More's interpretation. Book titles and short phrases, however, usually go untranslated even when the context leaves the meaning unclear. Undoubtedly, More was able to devote only a small part of his time and talent to the last of his controversial works. He completed the *Answer* in December 1533; a few months later, he was taken to the Tower for refusing to confirm the Act of Succession by oath.

III *Summary—The Polemical Books*

The years between 1523 and 1533 were filled with conflict and change for Thomas More and for all of Europe. During this time More wrote thousands of pages defending the unity, authority, and inspiration of the Catholic Church. His defense of its traditions stems from an absolute faith in the inspired nature of the Church: because Christ left the Holy Spirit to guide his Church, it cannot be permanently in error; because the inspired Church has traditionally held to certain doctrines, they must be true. The infallibility of the Church and the validity of the doctrines of purgatory and good works constitute the core of More's polemical theology; his defense of specific Church practices such as prayer, almsgiving, bodily affliction, penance, worshiping of saints and relics, and confession follows from his interpretation of those two doctrines. Likewise, his defense of the clergy and the real presence derives from his acceptance of the inspired nature of Church tradition.

Technically the individual polemical books resemble each other less than they do thematically, although certain stylistic habits pervade all the books, as does More's obvious desire to write in a way meaningful to the English reader whose education did not equip him to handle subtleties of language and thought. There is a noticeable deterioration between the *Dialogue concerning Tyndale* and the later writings, which make limited attempts at dramatic entertainment and often replace fictional exempla with bitter attacks on the personal morality of the Lutherans. Finally, however, the More of the earlier books reappears briefly in the *Debellation of Salem and Bizance* with witty satirical tales that seldom resort to the abuse of his enemies for humor.

CHAPTER 4

The Writer in the Tower

T HOMAS More's Tower writings constitute a profound meditation on Christian dying. Although they share many of the
qualities of prison and devotional literature in general, they also
reflect the unique experience of the writer. More knew his death
was imminent; it was not possible for him to think, as most of us do,
that death lay somewhere in the distant future.

Until recently, our main source for the prison writings and for information about their composition was the edition of More's
English works printed in 1557 by William Rastell. The works of
1533 - 35 as they appear in that edition are: *The Dialogue of Comfort*, "A Treatise to Receive the Blessed Body of our Lord,
Sacramentally and Virtually Both," "A Treatise upon the Passion of
Christ" in English, an English translation of the Latin "De Tristitia
Christi," and miscellaneous letters and devotions. Modern
scholarship suggests that the major Tower works were composed in
the following order: the English "Treatise upon the Passion," the
"Treatise to Receive the Blessed Body," *The Dialogue of Comfort*,
and the "De Tristitia Christi."

I *The Meditations on the Passion*

We know that at least part of the English "Treatise upon the
Passion"[1] was written before the other Tower works because a letter
from Thomas More to his secretary, John Harris, clearly indicates
that it was begun before his imprisonment.[2] He perhaps finished it
in the Tower, added the "Blessed Body" as a last chapter, and then,
at a time much closer to his death, wrote the unfinished Latin
treatise. Germain Marc'hadour has argued that both the "Treatise"
and the "Blessed Body" may have been written before More
entered the Tower as a continuation of the eucharistic controversy
begun in the *Answer to the Poisoned Book*—suggesting a grouping
which Garry Haupt calls the "late pre-Tower eucharistic works."[3]

112

The English treatise, written first, is the least meditative of the prison works; it is, rather than a meditation, a collection of instructions designed to teach the reader the proper attitude toward the events of Christ's life and the sacramental significance of those events. Emphasizing the effects of sinful pride and selfishness, it recounts the story of creation, the fall of Lucifer, and the fall of man. But early on, More begins preparing the reader for the Passion of Christ which offers the redeemed Christian greater joy than was possible before the fall of man and the angels. The "Treatise" is dominated by the consequences of the fall into pride—both the suffering and the redemption. It emphasizes mankind's total dependency on God's grace before the fall and on Christ's sacrifice after it; it treats the theological implications of the doctrine of original sin and of the conflict between the natural and the spiritual in man. More then begins his explication of the Passion of Christ, which he derives from the commentary on the four gospels by the medieval theologian and mystic John Gerson. He tells of the conspiracy against Christ, of the betrayal by Judas, and of Christ's isolation in suffering. About halfway through the treatise, More begins a long doctrinal treatment of the institution of the Eucharist; the treatise breaks off in the middle of a defense of the Catholic interpretation of the Sacrament.

Even though the "Treatise" is essentially a theological commentary which often deteriorates into the digressive ramblings of the later polemical books, at times we glimpse the fiction writer. More's native dramatic talent emerges in the descriptions of Adam and Eve (11 - 21) and Judas (75 - 83) and in the realistic depiction of the conflict between Christ and His enemies (68 - 75).

In the "Treatise," More presents two lectures on the Sacrament, dealing first with the institution and then the sacramental nature of the Eucharist. The treatise breaks off as the third lecture—which treats the proper way of receiving the Sacrament—begins. Louis Martz specualtes that the brief "Treatise on the Blessed Body" is, in fact, the completion of that lecture, which ends with a description of those who receive the Sacrament either sacramentally or spiritually; the "Blessed Body" finishes the sequence with a presentation of the third way of receiving the Sacrament—both sacramentally and spiritually.[4]

The "Blessed Body" looks forward to the meditativeness of the Latin treatise and the last book of the *Dialogue*, as do those parts of the "Treatise" in which More identifies with Christ in an effort to prepare himself for his own "passion." His description of the con-

spiracy against Christ suggests the behavior of More's own enemies.
And the "Treatise" is interspersed with prayers in which More
applies the circumstances of Christ's life to his own and prays that
he, like Christ, will be able to resist the temptation of devious advice and traps. In his emphasis on Christ's solitariness and self-
abnegation we see More preparing to renounce the world. Finally,
he points to Christ as an example of patience for all Christians who
suffer pain and death.

More's Latin treatise "De Tristitia Christi" (The Sadness of
Christ)[5] begins where the English treatises leave off, with the events
that follow the Last Supper. Except for a few short letters and
prayers, the "De Tristitia" is undoubtedly the last thing More
wrote; Rastell is explicit in saying that More left it unfinished
because he was deprived of pens and paper shortly before his death.
Perhaps the lapse in time explains the essential difference between
the two treatises. The Latin work is meditative rather than
theological in tone; now More is predominantly concerned with the
identification of the suffering Christian with the suffering Christ.
The theme of the Latin treatise is Christ's humanity, which teaches
man a way of suffering that transcends fear and pain. More relates
the experience of Christ to himself and to all who suffer, especially
for the faith, insisting that most of the martyrs and even Christ
knew fear, which rather than diminishing enhanced the significance
of their final courage. The disciples' abandonment of Christ shows
how they differed from Him in courage and establishes isolation as
one of the realities of death and martyrdom, one which must have
been especially painful for the gregarious More. He also considers
Christ's example in asking that the cup of suffering pass from him if
it be God's will. This act represents the ultimate surrender to God,
but also shows that the Christian is required to suffer pain and martyrdom only when happiness and life are in conflict with God's will.
Here More seeks in the events of Christ's Passion a solution to the
problems of his own conscience, for he knew that to seek martyrdom would be to fall to the sin of pride. Finally, like Christ, he asks
God to provide him with the knowledge to do His will.

Near the end of "De Tristitia," More returns briefly to the
problems of the world and reminds the reader of the present danger
from the Turks outside of Christendom and from the heretics within. He intermittently attacks the beliefs and motivations of the
Lutherans and warns Christians against betraying Christ for
Lutheranism. The treatise comes to a close with an explication of

the story of a young man who came wrapped in a sheet to Christ's capture. The last chapter ends abruptly: "after all the apostles had escaped by running away, after the young man who had been seized but could not be held had saved himself by his active and eager acceptance of nakedness, only then, after all these events, did they lay hands on Jesus" (625). Although the work is obviously not finished, Clarence Miller argues convincingly that it is "very nearly so."[6]

The "De Tristitia," like the other Tower works and like the earlier *Four Last Things,* is clearly in the tradition of late medieval meditative literature. But like all of More's Latin writing it is a work of Renaissance humanism as well and is probably addressed to a wider audience than are the English works. More's Latin style is as precise as ever, and the manuscript shows how meticulously he revised his final work. The book contains allusions to the classics and to the works of Erasmus and demonstrates the kind of textual analysis so important to Christian humanist scholarship. "De Tristitia" is unique to the extent that humanist interests and techniques are joined to the devotional.[7]

II A Dialogue of Comfort against Tribulation

The prison treatises are fragmentary, but the *Dialogue of Comfort*[8] is a complete, carefully organized narrative and a masterpiece of English devotional literature. The 1557 edition of More's English works states merely that Thomas More wrote the *Dialogue* in 1534 while he was a prisoner in the Tower. But we can be fairly safe in saying that it was composed between the spring and fall of 1534. Its intricate design and the superiority of the fiction indicate that More wrote the book during his early months in the Tower, when he still had the time and materials he needed to create a finished work of literature.[9] The *Dialogue* is almost altogether free of the signs of hasty composition that mar the later polemical works and parts of the prison treatises. Furthermore, the marked similarity in theme and style between Books I and II of the *Dialogue* and a letter of advice from More to his stepdaughter, Alice Alington, suggest that the *Dialogue* and the letter were written at about the same time. More and Margaret probably wrote the letter together in August 1534.[10] The tone of Book III, however, is closer to that of the treatises, especially the unfinished "De Tristitia," which was probably interrupted by the passing of the Acts of Supremacy and Treason in

November 1534. As we have seen, it was from this time that More
was deprived of his writing equipment and kept under a close
watch. The period of composition perhaps explains why, with the
exception of some of the letters, this is the only finished literary
product of the prison months. For a short while, More had the
leisure and the materials to do his best work. The *Dialogue*
demonstrates the final stage in the development of More's life and
art; here the pragmatic, witty More of Books I and II merges with
the contemplative More who reconciles himself to death in the final
book.

Yet even in his last meditative writings, More is aware of his
readers. The prison treatises and *Dialogue* as well as the letters
assume an audience. The English and Latin treatises teach the
reader how to interpret the events of Christ's life and death. The
Dialogue addresses a reader and ends with a prayer for him (423).
Many scholars, following the suggestion of the author's great-
grandson, Cresacre More, assume that More wrote the *Dialogue* to
prepare the minds of English Catholics for the impending persecution by the Protestants. Father Philip Hallett, in the "Introduction"
to his 1937 edition of the *Dialogue*, insists that More addressed the
book to his family and a small circle of intimates.[11] It seems likely
that Cresacre More is closer to the truth than Hallett, for the careful translation of most of the Latin in the *Dialogue* reveals More's
continuing awareness of the educational limitations of at least part
of his audience. Theological and narrative similarities between the
Dialogue and the polemical works further suggest that More intended all of his later English works for the general reader. In writing
the *Dialogue*, he probably had in mind not just his learned friends
and family but all the Catholics in England who needed support in
the immediate crisis of persecution and comfort in the ubiquitous
tribulations of sickness, solitude, and death.

The *Dialogue of Comfort*, like the *Utopia* and the *Dialogue concerning Tyndale*, takes the form of a debate between a spokesman
for More and a naive but benign opponent. It is set in Budapest,
Hungary, at the time of the Turkish invasion of 1528. Because of
the crisis, the young Vincent has come to his old, probably dying
uncle, Anthony, to ask his comfort and counsel for times of suffering. Anthony instructs Vincent in the nature of tribulation and the
kinds of benefits and encouragement to be gained from it. More
uses this situation to present the consolations of Christianity and
concludes the book with a meditation on the Passion of Christ—the

ultimate comfort to the Christian in the final agony of death. More embodies in Anthony the accumulation of his own experience. He draws on a background of literary humanism to create a polished dialogue that displays his best talents for allegory and fiction; he continues his defense of the Church by emphasizing the comfort inherent in Catholic doctrine; finally, he incorporates into the story his present need to reconcile himself to death, which he knows is imminent and which he fears will be painful.

More begins the *Dialogue* with a description of the suspenseful situation in Hungary. The first speech sets the tone of urgency that pervades the book as Vincent tells his uncle his fears. He thinks such bad times are coming that the happiest people will be those who know they will soon die; those who need the greatest comfort and counsel are the ones who, like himself, think they "are lykely long to lyve here in wrechidnes" (3). In his introduction Vincent describes his uncle as virtuous and learned in the law of God and adds that Anthony's life, though long, has been dangerous (3 -4). Anthony's experience, virtue, and wisdom qualify him to give the kind of advice and comfort that Vincent and More's readers need. It is obvious that More is thinking of himself in the descriptions of Anthony and characteristic that he describes with a degree of immodesty a persona who represents himself. Although the protagonist stands for the author, More clearly intends him also to function as a fictional character in the narrative. In answering Vincent, Anthony establishes early his wit, his amiability, and his desire to offer his nephew what comfort he can; he hints that the dialogue will be concerned with theological as well as spiritual comforts. Vincent's response heightens the dramatic impact of the story by describing in some detail the dangers the Turk brings—imprisonment, torture, the imposition of a false faith, and exile. After further descriptions of the Turk, Anthony and Vincent begin the discussion of comfort in tribulation.

The *Dialogue of Comfort* starts with an elaborate introduction to the political and historical setting of the story but gives few details of the immediate surroundings. The first book presents Anthony's analysis of the good to be derived from suffering. As it ends, More returns the reader to the narrative with Vincent's apology for having kept his uncle so long. The two agree to meet again soon to treat the last kind of tribulation.

Book II expands the fiction; as he did in the *Tyndale*, here More arranges the books in a dramatic framework which he enlarges as each section begins and ends. At the beginning of Book II, he reveals that Anthony is living with family or friends who care for him, his "folk." Apparently, a few days have passed since the last conversation, and Vincent has returned in hopes of hearing Anthony's final comfort against tribulation. Anthony assures his nephew that the conversation itself is a comfort to him and jests about the verbosity of old men. He insists that he was so comforted by the last meeting that he is glad they did not finish the subject and so have an excuse for more talk.

In Book II, Vincent often functions as the naive opponent who asserts unacceptable solutions in order to give More's spokesman an opportunity to refute them—much as the Messenger does in the *Tyndale*. Vincent tells Anthony that their earlier discussion had comforted not only himself but also "some other of your frendes, to whom as my pore wit & remembrraunce wold serue me/I did/and not nedeles/report & reherse your most comfortable counsayle" (79). But before they begin again he insists that Anthony tell him when he is tired or in such pain that he wishes to end the discussion. Throughout their conversations, the two reveal their love and consideration for each other; Vincent always shows great respect for Anthony's wisdom, which he seeks at a time when he must suspect that his uncle is dying. Definite characteristics of Anthony's personality become clear: he is wise, learned, generous, a little too talkative, aware of his own faults, delighted with a "merry tale," and optimistic in the face of death, old age, and physical pain. A good example of Anthony's ironic characterization of himself occurs early in Book II. He says that if he grew weary at their last meeting it was probably because he talked too much. He promises that from here on Vincent will get to do half the talking himself. But this is a promise that More and his personae can never keep, for although Vincent talks a little more here than he did in Book I, Anthony's speeches still cover about 80 percent of the book. As in Book I, Vincent's comments often serve merely as foils to Anthony's arguments.

After a story by Vincent, also about a garrulous man, the two proceed with a consideration of those who seek worldly relief from tribulation. More continues his habit of reminding the reader of the dialogue's fictional framework: Anthony interrupts his comments at one point to say that after a few more words they will go in to dinner (173). The "few words" take more than ten pages before he concludes with the suggestion that dinner be served, only to discover that it has already come. It has probably been waiting for them for some time, and Vincent is quick to encourage his uncle to stop long enough to eat the meal (186 - 87). It looks as if, for the time, at least, Vincent has had enough of the one-sided dialogue. The two part for Anthony to take his customary nap, which he insists will not be long since he wants to have the rest of "this long day" to devote to the most terrifying tribulation of all—that which comes with the temptations of persecution for the faith.

When Book III opens, Vincent has returned to his uncle much alarmed by a rumor that the great Turk is preparing a huge force of troops. He of course fears that the enemy is on its way to Budapest and that the temptations and torments which he and Anthony were to discuss are now imminent. Anthony tries to comfort his nephew with the hope that the rumor is false but admits that the Turk is likely at some time to come not only to Hungary but to all of Christendom. Finally, the treatment of suffering in persecution begins with additional urgency as Anthony insists that every Christian must be constantly prepared for the possibility of this kind of tribulation. The comfort in persecution is dominated by Anthony's insistence that the reward for faithfulness outweighs the suffering of fear, pain, and loss of life. After a lengthy consideration of the joys of heaven and the agony of Christ's Passion, Anthony brings the discussion abruptly to an end.

The *Dialogue* is a comfort and instruction for those in tribulation, a meditation on death, and a dramatic narrative depicting the affectionate relationship of two vividly portrayed personalities. The characterization of Anthony and Vincent is not, however, limited to the sections that frame the three books. Throughout the *Dialogue*, More reveals the individuality of the two men, devoting special attention to Anthony. Most exchanges between the two, however, give the reader insight into both characters. For example, in Book III, Anthony insists that Vincent act out the part of a rich man who wants to keep his goods while Anthony continues to refute his reasoning. This passage makes obvious just how pertinent the humorous play-acting can be as Anthony frustrates the solemnn Vincent into begging to be released from his role. Another exchange in Book III offers an even better example of Anthony's jocular treatment of the earnest, pedantic Vincent and demonstrates More's facility in using Socratic debate for the purposes of fiction as well as argument. Vincent describes the pains of imprisonment and says that he knows hardly anyone who is in prison. But after many pages of questions, answers, and examples Anthony succeeds in convincing his nephew that all men are prisoners in a world of pain, in bondage to sin, and sentenced to die at any time (275 - 76).

Anthony's tendency to make ironic comments about his own behavior is significant to a consideration of the polemical element in the *Dialogue of Comfort*. Book II begins with his portrayal of himself as a foolish, talkative old man who harmlessly makes promises he does not keep. The same kind of irony pervades the *Dialogue* in connection with Anthony's comments on Lutheranism. After denying that he is going to contend with the Lutherans, Anthony devotes most of Book I to topics bearing on his defense of the Church and summarizes the book with a statement that encompasses most of the important elements in his polemical position (75 - 77). Similarly, in Book II, after declaring that he will not dispute with the Lutherans, Anthony goes on to defend traditional Church interpretations of the scriptures on the grounds that it seems unlikely to him that these "new men" (the Lutherans) could have discovered in the scriptures any truths unknown to the fathers of the Church. Anthony makes a typically sardonic comment about the "new men" who think they have found an easy way to heaven and adds that he would not advise anyone to follow their way because it may not be sure, and the way of willing tribulation through penance is (98 - 99). Anthony says he will not dispute with the Lutherans but what follows is a thorough rebuttal of their position. Furthermore, the pages preceding Anthony's comment satirize a reforming preacher and defend fasting, penance, and bodily affliction (92 - 98). Later, Anthony makes a similar statement about his refusal to debate with those who say that because God can hear all prayers himself there is no need to pray to saints and to the dead (155 - 56). As usual, after asserting that he will not argue a particular issue, Anthony indulges in More's favorite methods of polemical debate with an appeal both to the scriptures and to the authority of the Church. More's defenders of the Church often use the same kind of ironic denial in the earlier works.

In addition to dialogue, narrative, and characterization, More makes skillful fictional use of dramatic tales and humorous anecdotes as exempla in the *Dialogue of Comfort*. One of the best of Anthony's illustrative stories and one of the most characteristic of More is Mother Maud's satirical tale concerning the relative scruples of the wolf and the ass. The priest in the tale is a fox, Father Reynard, in whom More portrays those clergymen who are being influenced by Lutheranism. The tale is also critical of the fox's two parishioners, the ass and the wolf. The wolf's conscience is not scrupulous enough and the ass's is too scrupulous; thus they both fail to realize the benefits of the penance they receive at confession. In telling this story, More demonstrates his talents for narration, humor, and satire as well as his ability to act as both critic and defender of the Church (112 - 21).

One of Vincent's tales is aimed at the Church establishment and Cardinal Wolsey. It tells of a great churchman who, having delivered a speech, cannot wait to hear his audience praise it and bluntly brings the subject up at dinner. When he asks the diners what they think of his speech, everything stops and each begins to ponder how he can most flatter the churchman. Vincent, who is one of the guests, is pleased with his praise until he is outdone by an unlearned priest. He comments that even one with a "right mean wit" can come to be skillful in a craft to which he has devoted his whole life—in this case, the craft of flattery. But he vows that next time he will speak in Latin and thus outshine the priest, who does not know Latin at all. But the experienced priest wins again:

for whan he saw that he could find no wordes of prayse that wold passe all that had bene spoken before all redy/the wily fox wold speke neuer a word, but as he that were ravishid vnto havyn ward, with the wonder of the wisedome & eloquence that my lordes grace had vttrid in that oracion, he fet a long sigh with an oh fro the bottom of his brest, & held vpp both his handes, & lyft vpp his hed, & cast vpp his yien into the welkyn, and wept/(215 - 16)

In the *Dialogue*, More achieves the combination of instruction and entertainment that he attempts in the earlier English books. Here he employs the techniques of fiction extensively and justifies his use of such "pleasant talking" in serious writing. Vincent questions Anthony about the enjoyment of storytelling, which he thinks his uncle may consider too worldly a pleasure. As for himself he sees no harm in a tale that gives a man courage and comfort in tribulation: "For a mery tale with a frend, refresheth a man much/& without any harm lightith his mynd & amendith his courage & his stomake/so that it semeth but well done to take such recreacion" (82). Anthony's point of view is more circumspect, but he too thinks a "merry tale" serves its purpose:

But thus much of that mater suffisith for our purpose/that where as you demaund me whether in tribulacion men may not sometyme refresh them selfe with worldly myrth & recreacion/I can no more saye/but he that can not long endure to hold vpp his hedd & here talkyng of hevyn except he be now & than betwene (as though hevyn were hevynes) refreshid with a folish mery tale/there is none other remedy, but you most let hym haue yt/better wold I wish it but I can not help it.

How be it let vs by myne advise at the lest wise, make these kyndes of recreacion as short & seld as we can/let them serue vs but for sawce & make them not our meate/and let vs pray vnto god & all our good frendes for vs, that we may fele such a savour in the delite of hevyn/that in respect of the talkyng of the ioyes therof, all worldly recreacion be but a grief to thinke on/And be sure Cosyn that yf we myght ones purchase the grace to come to that poynt/we neuer of worldly recreacion had so much comfort in a yere, as we shuld fynd in bethynkyng vs of hevyn in lesse than halfe an howre//(84 - 85)

Anthony, probably speaking for More, admits that he himself takes great pleasure in tales and merry talk but insists that the only real justification for illustrative anecdotes is that they hold the attention of listeners and readers who cannot tolerate long periods of devotion and study.

For the first time in many years More is at his best with dialogue, exempla, satire, and irony. The *Dialogue* also demonstrates his talent for allegory and analogy, especially in the long-foreshadowed development of the figure of the Turk. From the beginning of the sixteenth century, thoughtful European Christians, including the humanists, were alarmed by the Turkish forces moving across Europe; it is not surprising that Thomas More, like many of his contemporaries, chose the Turk to personify the enemy of Christ on earth.[12] Here, as in the polemical works, the Turk often represents either a general fictitious enemy or Suleiman I, the real historical leader of the Turkish invaders. Now, however, the figure of the Turk frequently functions as an expanded metaphor representing either Henry VIII, Lutheranism, or Henry as a political power allied to the Lutherans. By Book III, all facets of the metaphorical Turk combine to become one figure—the archetypal enemy of Christ. Often the figure of the Turk clearly refers to some aspect of More's relationship to Henry, especially in his association with Lutheranism (190 - 99, 200 - 201, 224 - 25, 226 - 27, 231 - 35, 280 - 81). Early in Book III, Anthony answers Vincent's naïve faith in the Turk's promises with a description of the Turk that suggests Henry's treatment of More and associates the Turk, Henry, with the false sect of Mahomet, Lutheranism (190 - 95). Anthony explains to Vincent that the Turk keeps his promises only when it is to his ad-

vantage and makes other charges which recall More's experience
with Henry and the "false sect" of Lutheranism. There are other
sections that plainly associate the Turk with Henry VIII. More
alludes to Henry's proclivity for senseless wars as well as his lack of
self-control in his personal life when he describes the Turk as one
who aspires to rule many realms despite his inability to control his
own kingdom and his own life (224 - 25). The references to those
who suffer poverty at the hands of the Turk for a refusal to deny the
faith appear even more topical than these when we remember
More's privation after his refusal to conform to the king's wishes.
Anthony assures Vincent that the true Christian will not compromise, for one's response to the temptation to keep his worldly
goods will "shew the faynid fro the trew myndid" (226). Shortly
after this comment, More again alludes to the Turk's failure to keep
his promises in another reference that suggests More's relationship
with Henry (231).

The *Dialogue* also associates the Turk with those who by means
of false testimony and the threat of a painful death attempted to
force More to abandon his conscience. But as Book III progresses,
the Turk is increasingly associated with the Lutherans. From the
beginning of the 1530s, Henry's relationship with the Reformers
was one of encouragement. Many allusions to Henry VIII in the
Dialogue reveal More's conception of him as the leader of a "false
sect." In telling of a merchant who was duped by the Sultan of
Syria, Anthony reveals the predicament of those who are tempted
by the promises of the Turk to hold on to their wealth. As he concludes the tale, he links the Turk with a "false sect." Here the
Turk's malice stems from his affiliation with that malicious religion:
"Wene you now my lord, that Sowdane & this Turke being both of
one false sect/you may not fynd them both like false of their
promise" (232). Other references indicate that persecution by the
Turk is due to religious inclinations and animosities. And Vincent
makes it clear that the Christian's keeping his possessions may depend upon his willingness to renounce his faith (228). Thus the
Turk comes to represent King Henry VIII, and the political power
of Lutheranism, and finally all God's enemies on earth. [13]

The construction of the *Dialogue of Comfort* reflects the two
themes that dominate the last years of More's life. In it we see the
public More, still defending the authority and viability of the
Catholic Church, but also the private person increasingly absorbed
in spiritual contemplation. It shows More fluctuating between his

great love for life and the need to prepare himself for death. Ultimately, he resolves the conflict as he moves away from earthly concerns toward union with Christ. Books I and II are dominated by the problems and pleasures of this world; Book III, by the spirit of medieval mysticism.

The consolation of the first two books of the *Dialogue* is essentially the comfort inherent in the community and authority of the Church. Book I begins with a statement of the premise that controls the first part of the *Dialogue* as well as all of More's polemical works—the source of all comfort and guidance in life is the Church and its traditions as they are inspired by the Holy Spirit. Anthony answers Vincent's request for comfort with the assertion, which he will reiterate throughout the book, that the only real comfort in tribulation lies in the knowledge of God's presence in the inspired Church (4 - 5). The consolation Anthony gives is that which More has been offering for years, the comfort that comes with belief in the traditional doctrines of the Church and in the presence of the Holy Spirit. As might be expected from the foregoing study of the polemical works, More moves from a statement of the inspired nature of the Church into an explanation and defense of Church traditions and practices. But from the beginning he carefully intertwines polemic and meditation.

Book I is a detailed description of suffering and the possibilities of comfort. In the analysis of tribulation, More insists that suffering should be welcomed because it is "medicinable" and serves the sufferer in three ways: it may be "medicinable" in paying for past sins; it may become "medicinable" in preventing sins that might otherwise be committed; it may be better than "medicinable" because it increases the possibilities of reward in heaven (23 - 24). The first book of the *Dialogue* is a consideration of the medicinal value of tribulation. But the discussion becomes in effect a justification of the doctrine of purgatory and the traditional kinds of good works associated with the remittance of sin. More builds his argument for the welcoming of tribulation on the premises that because God never punishes sin twice and always rewards good works, suffering on earth alleviates suffering in purgatory and stores up reward in heaven. He particularly emphasizes the doctrine of purgatory as it relates to the kind of tribulation that mitigates suffering for past sins. In proving that suffering is beneficial, More makes much of the dangers inherent in continual prosperity or happiness; since none is sinless, the absence of tribulation in this life means greater suffering in the next.

Book I is theological and polemical to the extent that More bases the consolation on his belief in Church doctrines concerning purgatory and upon his faith in rewards for such good works as penance and confession. It becomes increasingly controversial in tone and technique as Vincent reminds Anthony that now some people actually deny the doctrine of purgatory, and thus take all the meaning out of his case for the benefits of suffering. Here Vincent, playing the "straight man" to More's spokesman, asserts the Lutheran denial of purgatory, voluntary suffering, and the efficacy of good works. Though Anthony declares that he will not argue with the Lutherans, he proceeds with a vigorous defense of purgatory and good works, supporting his argument with the authority of the Church fathers and the scriptures (37 - 40). Thus the comfort of Book I rests on More's two major theological premises, that the inspired Church cannot be permanently in error and that the doctrines of purgatory and good works are essential beliefs for faithful Christians. Also implicit in More's treatment of the comforts of the Church is the preeminence of faith. Finally, the comfort of tribulation that constitutes Book I is the comfort of the traditional Church.

The idea of the Church as the ultimate source of comfort contributes to the thematic unity of the *Dialogue*. Other devices that appear in Book I demonstrate More's extreme care in organizing the three sections of the book. One such device develops out of the three-part treatment of the medicinal nature of tribulation. The third kind of suffering is that of the man so good that he has no sins to pay for in purgatory; his comfort comes from the knowledge that he is storing up special reward in heaven. More gives his third medicinal comfort cursory treatment in Book I because he is saving it for Book III where he will incorporate it into his meditation on martyrdom. He deliberately postpones the discussion of the suffering that is better than medicinal and foreshadows the attention it will receive later, thereby binding Book I to the main issues of Books II and III. Similarly, Book II describes three kinds of tribulation. They are tribulation willingly taken, tribulation willingly suffered, and tribulation that cannot be avoided (86 - 87). Here also More abbreviates the matter he is saving for Book III. In Book I, he postpones the discussion of the kind of suffering which, instead of paying for sins, gains glory in heaven; here he postpones the discussion of the kind of tribulation that cannot be avoided. He then divides tribulation willingly suffered into the four temptations of Psalm 90 and again postpones the discussion of the last one until Book III, where he will consider it—the open temptation of the

devil at midday—as part of the comfort to the Christian who suffers
death and torment for his faithfulness. The tribulation that is better
than medicinal, the tribulation that cannot be avoided, and the
temptation of the devil at midday all turn out to be aspects of the
same thing—suffering for the faith. The foreshadowing indicates
that More designed the *Dialogue* so that the divisions of tribulation
in Books I and II would come together in Book III with his consideration of the painful, shameful death of the martyr. Nowhere in
his writing does More better demonstrate his dramatic sense of tim-
ing and suspense than in his prison dialogue.

More's careful linking of the ideas in Book II to those in Book I
and Book III is clearest in the analysis of the temptations of tribulation not willingly taken but willingly endured. One temptation he
defines as the secret wiles, or "trains," of the devil; the other, as the
devil's open attack. More has Anthony relate that there are comforts
in all kinds of temptation, that victory over them gains eternal
reward, and that, in fact, there is no real possibility of defeat for one
who is confident of God's protection. It is here that he first introduces the verses from Psalm 90: "*Scapulis suis obumbrabit tibi,
& sub pennis eius sperabis:* with his sholders shall he shadow the, &
vnder his fethers shalt thow trust (103);*" the devil is powerless
against God's strong shield, or pavis. He then divides willingly suffered tribulation into the four temptations described in the Psalm.
The first is the night's fear, or temptation deriving from fear and
impatience. The second, the arrow flying in the day, is the temptation to pride in worldly possessions. And the third, business walking
in the darkness, is the temptation to worldliness and covetousness.
Finally, there is the invasion of the devil at midday or the direct
temptation of persecution (105 - 106). More predicts the extensive
treatment in Book III of this last and worst danger when he has
Anthony say to Vincent: "& than will we call for our dener levyng
the last temptacion that is to wit/*Ab incursu & demonio
meridiano*/from the incursion & the devill of the midd day/till after
none/& than shall we therwith god willyng make an end of all this
mater" (165).

In Book II, More builds his theological concerns into the description of the possibilities of comfort in tribulation. He introduces the
dominant issues of the Church controversy early when Anthony tells
Vincent of the benefits of good works to the man who chooses suffering in order to pay for sins or to win rewards in heaven (87 - 90).
Vincent immediately reminds his uncle of the Lutheran opinion

that since salvation is by faith alone, the man who suffers for his sins does "playn iniury to the passion of christ/by which onely are our sinnes forgevyn frely without any recompence of our own" (93). He illustrates the Lutheran position with the satirical tale of the Saxony preacher and Anthony responds with one of the main points in his defense of Catholic beliefs—although the Church requires good works, it has never maintained that one is saved by deeds without faith (93 - 95). Against the words of the Lutheran preacher, Anthony defends his original statement about the importance of penance and clarifies his stand on the relationship between faith and works. He continues his defense by bombarding his opponents with the authority of the scriptures and the Church fathers (95 - 96) and concludes with a direct refutation of the Lutheran position (98 - 99).

More then turns to the first of the temptations of willingly suffered tribulation, the night's fear or pusillanimity, and continues his opposition to Lutheran opinions. The tale of Father Reynard illustrates the temptation of the too scrupulous conscience and criticizes a priest who has betrayed his flock for the new beliefs. More ends the discussion of this temptation by recommending the comfort available in the sacraments of the Church: "And therfor as I say who so hath such a trowble of his scrupulouse conscience: let hym for a while forbere the iugement of hym selfe, & folow the counsayle of some other, whom he knowith for well lernid & vertuouse, & specially in the place of confession/For there is god specially present with his grace assistyng his sacrament" (121). Similarly, he offers the strength and support of the Church to the man who is tempted to suicide (155 - 56). Thus, although he presents a complex analysis of suffering and temptation in Book II, he repeatedly offers one solution to the problems of tribulation—the consolation inherent in Church customs and beliefs.

An examination of the structure of Books I and II of the *Dialogue* suggests not the digressive repetitiveness of a hastily composed prison work but a complex design systematically foreshadowing the climactic final book. The unity is emphasized by the pervasive intertwining of the theological and consolatory motifs.

Finally, in Book III, the long-promised discussion of Christian martyrdom unites the comfort that is better than medicinal (Book I) with the comfort for unavoidable and open temptation (Book II). Here the two major themes come together in the development of

THOMAS MORE

128

the figure of the Turk and in the meditation on Psalm 90. The culmination of the hortatory theme appears mainly in the expanded figure of the Turk, which as a metaphor for Lutheranism and for Henry VIII has come to stand for all Christ's earthly enemies. Here More looks once more at the theological concerns of the preceding years. But the comfort motif culminates in his portrayal of the suffering Christian who transcends the temptations posed by his enemies and joins himself to Christ in death. At the same time that consolation and theology merge in the encounter between the Turk and Christ, the divisions of comfort come together in the consideration of martyrdom. By Book III, the *Dialogue* has become a complex treatise in which the mystical unification of the martyr with Christ encompasses and transcends the worldly problems and controversies of Books I and II. All converge in the consideration of Christ's Passion, with the Turk representing the enemies of both the suffering Christ and the suffering Christian. The transformation of the Turk is complete by the time Anthony proves that "the consideracion of the paynefull deth of Chryst, is sufficient to make vs content to suffre paynefull deth for his sake" (312). The Turk, who has come to stand for all the forces that tempt the Christian to forget the love of Christ and the power of God is but a shadow; still there is danger for the Christian in the possibility that he will allow the Turk and the devil to tempt him to value worldly comforts more than he fears eternal damnation. When the *Dialogue of Comfort* ends, Christ has overcome the problems and conflicts of the world which so dominate Vincent's thoughts and Anthony's comfort in the first two books.[14]

III *Devotions and Miscellaneous Works*

In addition to the treatises and the *Dialogue of Comfort*, the 1557 edition includes a collection of devotional writings and letters. We also have from the prison months More's annotated *Prayer Book*—a volume containing the *Psalter* and a *Book of Hours*. Along the margins of the *Book of Hours*, a popular type of primer devoted to the services and prayers of the Virgin Mary, is written in More's hand this prayer which first appeared in print in 1557 under the title "A Godly Meditation":

GEue me thy grace good Lorde
to set the worlde at nought.

To set my mynde fast vppon the.

And not to hange vppon the blast of mennes mouthes.

To be content to be solitary.

Not to long for worldly company.

Lytle & litle vtterly to cast of ye worlde.

And ridde my mynde of alll the busynesse therof.

Not to long to heare of any worldlye thynges.

But that the hearyng of worldly fantasyes maye be to me displeasant.

Gladly to be thynking of god.

Piteously to call for his helpe.

To leane vnto the coumforte of God.

Busily to labour to loue hym.

To knowe myne owne vilitee & wretchednes.

To humble and meken my self vnder the myghty hand of god.

To bewayl my sinnes passed.

For the purgyng of them, pacientlye to suffer aduersitie.

Gladly to beare my purgatorye here.

To be ioyful of tribulacions.

To walke the narowe way that leadeth to lyfe.

To beare the crosse with Christ.

To haue the laste thynge in remembrance.

To haue euer afore myne eye, my death, that is euer at hande.

To make death no straunger to me.

To foresee and consider the euerlasting fier of hell.

To pray for pardone before the iudge come.

To haue continually in mind, the passion that Christ suffred for me.

For his benefites vncessantly to giue him thankes.

To bye the time again, that I before haue lost.

To abstaine from vaine confabulacions.

> To eschewe light foolishe mirthe and
> gladnes.
> Recreacions not necessary to cut of.
> Of worldly substance, frendes, liber-
> tye, life, and al, to sette the losse at
> right nought, for the winning of Christ.
> To thinke my most enemies my beste
> frendes.
> For the bretherne of Ioseph, coulde
> neuer haue done him so much good with
> their loue and fauor, as they did him w^t
> their malice and hatred.
> These mindes are more to be desired of
> euery man, than all the treasure of all the
> princes and kinges christen & heathen,
> were it gatherd and layde together
> all vppon one heape. [15]

The "Meditation" gives us an intimate glimpse of More's thoughts as he approached death; it is a finished poem which distills the ideas and emotions of all the prison writings. Increasingly, More acknowledges and even welcomes the painful, frightening realities of his situation as he focuses on surrendering his will to God. Although, as he tells us, More desired the spiritual opportunities that accompanied imprisonment, he was painfully aware of the abundance he left behind.

Two passages in the "Meditation" are especially significant in relation to the *Dialogue of Comfort*. Lines 22 - 28 are reminiscent of the *Dialogue* and suggest that the sections on purgatory and persecution were written partly in response to More's own need for encouragement and comfort. Here he prays that he may be joyful in the suffering which allows him to bear his purgatory for past sins now rather than later. And when in lines 55 and 56 he asks for the generosity to "thinke my most enemies my beste frendes," we suspect he is thinking of my political and religious enemies who figure so prominently in the last years of his life and in parts of the *Dialogue*. Ultimately, the "Meditation," like the other Tower works, shows More "casting off the world" in order "to bear the cross with Christ."

The notes in the margin of the *Psalter* further elucidate More's thoughts during the prison months. A number of marginal references to the Turk recall the significance of the metaphor in the

Dialogue. The annotations also reflect More's preoccupation with the temptations of suffering, imprisonment, and solitude. And, as in the *Dialogue*, he considers both the problems of the scrupulous conscience and the benefits of tribulation. Finally, the marginalia show More steeling himself against the assaults on his conscience. Two themes pervade the *Dialogue* and the notes in the *Psalter*—how the faithful Christian is to bear tribulation in general and how he is to behave when tempted to betray the faith.

The 1557 edition includes prayers that Rastell says More wrote after he was condemned to die. Now he prays to be joined to Christ in suffering and to "haue recourse to that great feare and wonderfull agonye, that thou my sweete sauiour hadst at the mount of Oliuete before thy moste bitter passion, and in the meditacion therof, to conceue ghostly coumfort and consolacion profitable for my soule."[16]

Considering the devotional nature of his last books, it may surprise some readers that the works of More's imprisonment include two short ballads, "Davy the dicer" and "Lewis the lost lover." But a look at the poems reveals their thematic relationship to the other writing of those months. The playful "Davy" tells of a gambler who had long served Lady Luck and finally lost everything except the leisure to make rhymes. "Lewis the lost lover" is the more serious of the two and is written in the first person; it describes the writer's decision to trust God and the security of heaven rather than "ey flatering fortune," who is deceptive and always follows her calm with a storm. Both poems treat the contrast between the fickleness of fortune and the sureness of God, a subject which attracted More early in life and which understandably pervades the works of the prison years. There is, however, a notable difference in tone in the two poems. "Davy the dicer," like the first books of the *Dialogue of Comfort*, uses narrative and irony to reveal the folly of those who trust worldly good fortune. But the hero of "Lewis the lost lover" rejects fortune and surrenders to the will of God in the spirit of the more devotional of the prison writings, including the final book of the *Dialogue*.

IV *Letters*

Finally, no consideration of More's prison works should overlook his last letters. As the early letters reflect the literary and historical significance of More's humanistic involvement, the later ones reveal the personal meaning of the events that precede his death. It is not coincidental that most of the extant letters of 1534 and 1535 are in English rather than Latin, for now, instead of writing self-consciously for literary and political purposes, More concentrates on the most intimate and relevant facts of his existence; the style is that of the king's "good servant," the friend, the father, and the dying Christian.

More wrote several letters to Thomas Cromwell and Henry VIII in the three months before his incarceration on April 17, 1534. The letters reflect the realities of More's life; he was facing false charges and knew that he would probably be imprisoned and put to death for his refusal to endorse the king's activities on behalf of the divorce. On February 1, he sent a letter to Cromwell declaring his innocence of any opposition to the king's affairs. When he learned that his name was included in the Bill of Attainder against the Nun of Kent and her adherents, he wrote Cromwell again, asking for a copy of the bill and an opportunity to discuss the matter with Henry in person. After being refused a hearing with the king, More could no longer doubt the dangers to himself and perhaps to his family. A few weeks later he sent Cromwell a long letter fully explaining the details of his position; he describes his relationship to the Nun and his absolute refusal to participate in her attack on the king. Here Thomas More the lawyer defends himself with the logical, forceful, sometimes angry, presentation of the facts in his favor. As the letter ends, he adds an emotional appeal. In a desperate attempt to rouse Cromwell's sense of justice and compassion, More reminds Cromwell that he, who has always been loyal to the king, writes his apology despite a painful heart condition.[17]

After More appeared before the commission investigating his involvement with the Nun of Kent, he wrote another letter to Cromwell and one to Henry. The letter to Henry is formal, reminding the king of More's loyalty and prudence in the past and referring to the recent letter to Cromwell; he does not defend his behavior in the letter to Henry because he thinks it inappropriate to argue and quibble with the king. The letter is straightforward and respectful, but terse in reminding Henry of his and More's past relationship.[18]

The last letter to Cromwell, however, is another legalistic and logical plea for justice. More writes as to an equal whom he hopes to persuade with reason; and he no longer conceals his impatience. He forcefully defends his actions concerning the Nun, the "great matter" of the king's marriage, and his alleged support of the Pope. Here, for the first time, he makes a direct claim on the king, reminding Cromwell that, soon after he became Chancellor, Henry had "declared vnto me that he wold in no wise that I shold other thing do or say therin, than vppon that that I shold perceive myn awne conscience shold serve me, and that I shold fyrst loke vnto God and after God vnto hym."[19] More could hardly have made his intentions any clearer. He had always put God and his conscience before the king, but the king before all else. These were the priorities for which he was ready to die.

The letters to Henry and Cromwell demonstrate More's talent for debate. And despite the seriousness of the subject, there are flashes or irony and humor. In the last letter, More cannot resist reminding Cromwell, and Henry, that he himself had doubted the primacy of the Pope as an institution of God before he read the king's own defense of the papacy in the book against Luther.[20]

The letters from the Tower are increasingly personal and show More moving away from the hope of altering his circumstances toward an acceptance of them. There are two letters of sympathy to Dr. Nicholas Wilson, who was also in the Tower for refusing the oath, and a letter of farewell to More's friend Antonio Bonvisi.[21] But most of the Tower letters are to his daughter Margaret, through whom he communicated with family and friends. During the first months in the Tower, More was allowed to see his family, to walk outside, and to go to Mass. His early letters reflect the relative freedom of his circumstances and his continued good spirits, even optimism. The first letter, sent to Margaret soon after More was taken to the Tower, describes the investigation at Lambeth. It is a dramatic account of the sophistry of his inquisitors and the antics of those who swore the oath. In it, More reveals his attitude toward the oath that accompanied the Act of Succession, one which he reiterates in subsequent letters: his conscience will not allow him to take the oath although he remains in all things loyal to the king and never will, as he never had, interfere with the conscience of anyone who disagrees with him.[22]

At some time during the first month of More's imprisonment, Margaret apparently wrote to her father trying to persuade him to change his position. Although Rastell's introduction to More's answer insists that Margaret wrote the letter merely to gain Cromwell's confidence and further permission to see her father, More's reply sounds as if he thought her letter was a serious attempt to change his mind. In his sorrowful and surprised response, More reprimands Margaret for trying to persuade him to forsake his beliefs. The letter ends in the devotional tone of the prison books.[23]

More's displeasure, however, did not stop family efforts to save him. At the end of the summer, his stepdaughter Alice Alington managed to talk with Henry's new Lord Chancellor, Thomas Audley, on her stepfather's behalf. Alice described the conversation to Margaret in a letter that Margaret showed to her father. Together father and daughter wrote a reply in the form of a dialogue which gives us one last example of More's skill in using that genre to instruct his readers. In it, Margaret acts the part of More's tempters, whom he refutes with anecdotes and tales. He uses his best techniques of debate—logic, exempla, humor, irony, satire, and the invocation of authorities—and concludes by insisting that regardless of what others do or think, he will abide by his conscience and endure what he must, comforted by the spiritual benefits of imprisonment.[24]

In the last letters to Margaret, More acknowledges the danger to himself and the irreconcilability of his differences with the king. He often expresses his willingness to die, his unwillingness to alter his position, and his affection for his family. At one point, he says that the only worldly consolation he misses is the opportunity for talk with his friends and family. He encourages them all and assures them that his way is not the only way, that two people may be of different consciences and still be "safe ynough before God" if both are true to their beliefs.[25] These last letters recount More's examinations in the Tower by the king's councilors; he states his position for the last time, reminding his interrogators that he has already declared himself to both Henry and Cromwell and that he never again intends to meddle with the world but to concentrate his "hole study . . . vppon the passyon of Chryst and myne owne passage owt of thys worlde."[26] The last letter to Margaret was written the day before More's execution and is a simple farewell to those closest to him.

V *"Thy Grace to Set the World at Nought"*

The Tower works taken together with some of the earlier books, especially the *Life of John Picus* and the *Four Last Things*, reflect the pervasive influence of Christian mysticism in More's writing. R. W. Chambers has already demonstrated the connection between

Thomas More and the English devotional writers of the Middle Ages. More would have known the works of such writers as Richard Rolle, Walter Hilton, Nicholas Love, Dame Juliana of Norwich, Margery Kempe, the translator of the *Imitation of Christ*, and the authors of the *Cloud of Unknowing* and the *Ancren Riwle*—if not in his father's home, then certainly in the Charterhouse at London.[27] We know how much More valued such devotional writing from a comment in the *Confutation*. There he suggests that his readers commit themselves to prayer, meditation, and the reading of English books of devotion rather than to books of controversy like his and Tyndale's (37). He recommends specifically Nicholas Love's *Mirror of the Blessed Life of Jesus Christ*, Walter Hilton's *Scale of Perfection*, and the English translation of the *Imitation of Christ*.

Before considering More as a devotional writer in the tradition of Christian mysticism, it is necessary to define that tradition in some detail. Chambers avoids the word mysticism and discusses More in the wider genre of English devotional literature. The term itself is troublesome for two reasons: twentieth-century usage is quite broad, giving the word connotations inappropriate to this discussion; and in the sixteenth century the words "devotion," "meditation," and "contemplation" were all used to describe the concentration of attention on spiritual realities.

Although we are especially concerned with More's relationship to Christian mysticism, the tradition precedes Christianity. Western literature acquires its earliest understanding of the mystical approach from Plato and the Neoplatonists, who established the essential steps of Purification, Contemplation, and Unification. The early Church fathers, deeply influenced by Neo-platonic mysticism, adhered to the three stages but made the life of Christ the object of their contemplation. Christian mysticism became the journey to God through Christ.

In his English writings, More inundates the reader with references to the thinkers of the early Church—St. Clement, St. Augustine, St. Gregory, and the Pseudo-Dionysius. The patristic writers who shaped his theology undoubtedly constitute one of the major sources of the contemplative element in his thought. The mystical works of the early Church are marked by the struggle of purgation and by the movement toward illumination through the contemplation of Christ and creation.

More is also indebted to the writers of the twelfth century, the second great era of Christian mystical writing, often drawing on the

opinions and words of St. Bernard and St. Bonaventure. Medieval
writers systemized and expanded the methods of patristic
mysticism. In the purgative phase, they stress active good works and
charity as well as purification of the soul, and now the illuminative
stage, which initiates Contemplation, clearly marks a new
awareness of the possibility of ascent to God. But what is newest
and most important in medieval mysticism is the unique place given
to contemplating the humanity of Christ. Thus the contemplative
way takes two directions—the Christocentric and the Theocentric.
In the Christocentric method, concentration on Christ's life, his
teachings, and his suffering leads the way to God. Theocentric contemplation is based on the Platonic approach to God through
meditation on his creatures. From the Middle Ages the Christocentric method dominated Christian mysticism. This is the tradition
that produced the great period of devotional writing in England.

Our earliest significant example of mysticism in More occurs in
the *Life of John Picus,* written for a nun at a time when More was
probably considering the contemplative life for himself. The book
begins with an autobiography epitomizing the temptations and
problems of the active life. The "Letters" and the "Commentary on
Psalm 15" further treat the problems of the world and recommend a
life of contemplation and study. The commentary calls to mind
purgation with its treatment of the spiritual impediments that must
be removed if one is to approach God. And the description of the
goodness of God, which "is not the goodness of any creature" (376),
suggests Theocentric contemplation. The commentary ends praising God and recalling the sacrifice of Christ.

"The Twelve Rules of Spiritual Battle" are greatly expanded in
More's translation and are, as the title suggests, contemplative in
nature. The first three stanzas stress the difficulty of the earthly
struggle, suggesting purgative self-conquest. Rules No. 4 and No. 5
are Christocentric admonitions that the reader conform to the examples of the suffering Christ. "The Twelve Rules" follow the
medieval writers in concentrating on the example of Christ's
physical pain, His shame, and His humility in accepting the vileness
and mutability of the human condition. The "Rules" are a grim account of the Christian's hard battle against "filthy sin." The tone of
"The Twelve Weapons of Spiritual Battle" is similar to that of the
"Rules." Both display elements of purgation and Christocentric
contemplation.

More's expansion of the Platonic "Twelve Properties of a Lover" follows the "Weapons." He translates Picus's twelve phrases into twenty-six stanzas that compare physical love and lovers to their spiritual counterparts. Here we see evidence of the illuminative stage as More admonished God's lovers to suffer anything rather than be separated from the beloved and so procure: "After this valley dark, the heavenly light, And of his love the glorious blessed sight" (390). The "Properties" stress the spiritual lover's overwhelming desire to be with God in prayer and meditation.

More's final selection, Picus's prayer unto God, becomes a thanksgiving for the grace that brings the writer, still so aware of his sinfulness, to a new level of intimacy with God. Again the language suggests illumination:

> Grant me, good Lord and Creator of all,
> The flame to quench of all sinful desire
> And in thy love set all mine heart afire. (396)

The *Life* and the selections that accompany it are in effect a sketch of the first stages of the Christian mystics' quest of communion with God.

The contemplative element emerges again in the *Four Last Things*. This fragment, which begins a meditation on the last things (death, doom, pain, and joy), suggests the purgative way in its consideration of the awful realities of earthly existence, realities mitigated only by self-conquest and good deeds. Here is the contemplative's acute consciousness of his unworthiness and of the struggle to strip away "those superflous, unreal, and harmful things" that prevent communion.[28] But again, joy accompanies purgation as More considers the pleasures which are the "very certain token that a penitent beginneth to profit and grow in grace and favour of God" (464). By meditating on the four last things one can "pull out these weeds of fleshly voluptousness" and "plant in their places, not only wholesome virtues but also marvellous ghostly pleasure and spiritual gladness, which in every good soul riseth of the love of God, and hope of heaven" (462 - 63). If he abandons sin and carnal pleasure, the Christian finds "sweetness, comfort, pleasure, and gladness" in the present life as well as in the world to come. The *Four Last Things* demonstrates the joy of contemplation, the greatest earthly pleasure, by showing how meditation on death, doom, and pain end in happiness.

The *Life* and the *Four Last Things* include passages reminiscent of the Christocentric contemplation so important in medieval mysticism, but it is not until he is writing in the Tower that More uses this method of meditation extensively. The illumination traditionally expressed itself in contemplation on the humanity and suffering of Christ and, to a lesser degree, in contemplation on the attributes of God; Christ as teacher and model becomes the way to God. Thus the Christian moves from identification with the humanity of Christ to an understanding of his divinity and finally to communion with God.

The English "Treatise" establishes the direction for all the prison works. It recounts the history of man—his creation, his fall, and his redemption through Christ—and makes Christ the model of virtue for fallen humanity. The "De Tristitia Christi," written nearer the time of More's death, uses the events of Christ's death as the ultimate example for the suffering Christian. More's concern here is that the troubled Christian identify with the suffering Christ. He depicts Christ's anguish—sorrow, isolation, pain, and fear—and His humility in assuming the human condition in words that often reflect More's own fear of the temptations of pain and death.

Both treatises and the *Dialogue of Comfort* attach great significance to Christ's Passion and death. The first two books of the *Dialogue* return to problems of the world, treating the issues of theology, politics, government, and the family, but Book III, dominated by Christ's victory over the Turk, becomes the culmination of the contemplative theme in the Tower works. Now, by concentrating on the life of Christ, More wipes out the Turk and with him the temptations that accompany wealth, fame, authority, fear, and shame. The remembrance of Christ's suffering, especially in physical pain and "bonddage," becomes the ultimate comfort in persecution for the faith and, finally, in all kinds of tribulation. The climactic last chapter is introduced by a statement that evokes the two major points in Christocentric contemplation—the importance of Christ's life as an example and the essentiality of the Christian's identifying with Christ's suffering: "Our hed is Christ/& therfor to hym must we be Ioynid/& as membres of his must we folow him/yf we will come thither. He is our Guyde . . . and he therfor that will enter in after . . . the same way that Christ walkyd, the same way must he walke. . . . Who can for very shame desire to entre into the kyngdom of Christ with ease, whan hym selfe entrid not into his own without payne" (311). What follows is an intimate meditation on the details and meaning of Christ's suffering.

The other Tower devotionals and letters also show More's moving away from the concerns of the world toward the rewards of contemplation. And Roper says that "In the tyme somewhat before his [More's] trouble, he wold talke with his wife and children of the ioyes of heuen and the paynes of hell, of the lyves of holy martires, of their greiuous martirdome, of their marvelous patiens, and of their passions and deathes that they suffred rather than they wold offend god."[29] After his imprisonment, More tells Margaret that the "feare of hel, the hope of heauen and the passion of Christ" assuage his fear of death and recommends that she also take comfort and direction from the remembrance of Christ's suffering.[30] And later he describes telling the king's councilors that he intends to spend the rest of his life "studying" the Passion of Christ and his own death.[31] Finally, the "Godly Meditation" epitomizes the intent of the Tower works as More prays for the grace to set the world at nought: "lytle & litle vtterly to cast of y^o world . . . to beare the crosse with Christ. To haue the laste thynge in remembrance."[32]

CHAPTER 5

Renaissance Man in the Twentieth Century

ASSESSING Thomas More's place in history and literature has become a complicated matter. Interpretations of More's life fluctuate with the times and are affected by attitudes toward his martyrdom, his sainthood, and his relationship to Henry VIII and to English Protestantism. Biographers and historians have seen Thomas More as a humanist scholar and reformer but also as a reactionary bigot, as a contributor to modern political thought, and as a profoundly conservative thinker deeply rooted in his medieval heritage. Scholarly estimates of his significance as a writer are similarly varied: in anthologies of English literature, More usually gets little space, yet R. W. Chambers and others see him as the father of modern English prose.[1]

I More's Life—Assessments

Thomas More's earliest biographers, Roper, Harpsfield, and Stapleton, tend to idealize More's character, to accentuate his spiritual life, and to focus more on his personality than on his writing. The tendency to simplify his complex life by concentrating on one aspect of it has continued among modern scholars.[2] Another perspective has tried to explain More in terms of what some historians see as his inexplicably paradoxical nature.[3] But if we augment the portraits of Roper, Harpsfield, and Stapleton with the More-Erasmus correspondence, we get a clearer and larger image of More—both as a human being and as a literary figure. From 1515, the letters of the two men reveal More's deep and enthusiastic involvement in the affairs of international humanism; letters to his family reflect his determination to apply the ideals of humanism to the education of the children in his household. Erasmus's famous description of More in a letter to Ulrich von Hutton (1519) shows us a witty man with normal conflicts and extraordinary energy for solving them. Erasmus mentions More's decision to marry rather than follow a religious vocation and demonstrates his dedication to family, friends, and work. We see someone who is moderate in the way he eats, drinks, dresses, and entertains himself but immoderate in his devotion to other people. Two years later a letter from Erasmus to William Budé emphasizes More's profound commitment to learning—for himself, his friends, and his children.[4]

Scholars continue to try to explain the intricacies of More's character and his career. R. W. Chambers interprets More's thought in terms of his medieval heritage. He attempts to place the essentially satiric fiction of the *Utopia* where it belongs in More's thinking and to show how More, a product of medieval stability, is affected by an age of transition: he "connects Medieval England with Modern England, and he connects England with Europe," and he links the literature of the sixteenth century with medieval devotional writing. According to Chambers, we misunderstand More when we forget that the "Utopian state, with its communism, its sacerdotalism, its love of beauty and of symbolic ritual, remains in touvch with the Middle Ages. The charges of inconsistency against More arise from our forgetting all this; from our forgetting that his life falls in this last age of English medieval Catholicism, and from our reading back, into his earlier writings, the experience, and even the propaganda of later generations."[5] He suggests that More's modern critics see contradictions in a set of commitments that were not in conflict in the milieu out of which they came. Thus, according to Chambers, More remains faithful to the conservative, medieval tradition to which he belonged.

Although Robert Bolt's orientation is modern, he too emphasizes the congruity of More's life and thinking. Bolt's play, *A Man for All Seasons*, pictures More as heroically consistent. Bolt has taken a man whom historians have viewed as "a bundle of antitheses" and made him a modern hero of wholeness who, despite his wide interests and zest for life, would not "retreat from that final area where he located his self."[6] For Bolt, the words for More are not paradox and contradiction but integrity and selfhood.

II *More's Works—Assessments*

The scholarly estimation of More's writing has been almost as diverse as that of his life. In his essay on "The Continuity of English

Prose," R. W. Chambers makes broad claims for More as a writer. He says that More took the traditions of medieval devotional writing and developed "an effective prose, sufficient for all the purposes of his time: eloquent, dramatic, varied. . . . More was the first man who possessed a prose style equal to all the needs of Sixteenth-Century England. . . . what England most needed was a prose style in which contemporary events were recorded in living and dramatic narrative."[7] For Chambers, More is not only the great "restorer" of English prose; he is also England's first great vernacular historian, her first and greatest writer of utopias, the greatest member of her first group of modern scholars, and one of the initiators of modern English drama.[8] Morean scholars seem to line up according to Chambers—either Thomas More is the father of modern English prose or he is not. Even the writers who precede Chambers fall into similar positions. James Mackintosh, writing in 1846, considered More to be the first writer of good English prose,[9] but George Saintsbury, fifty years later, thought the idea of More as the "father of English Prose" was absurd.[10] C. S. Lewis, like other recent scholars, questions Chambers's estimation of More's prose style:

Great claims have in modern times been made for More's English prose; I can accept them only with serious reservations. . . . The man who sits down and reads fairly through fifty pages of More will find many phrases to admire; but he will also find an invertebrate length of sentence, a fumbling multiplication of epithets, and an almost complete lack of rhythmical vitality. . . . There are no lightning thrusts: and, on the other hand, no swelling tide of thought and feeling. The style is stodgy and dough-like. As for the good phrases, the reader will already have divined their nature. They come when More is in his homeliest vein: . . . . They belong to the same world as his merry tales. Nearly all that is best in More is comic or close to comedy.[11]

More's early works have received varying degrees of scholarly attention, much of it devoted to the *Utopia*. The poems, the epigrams, and the Lucianic works are seen as products of More's apprenticeship in the humanities; the *Utopia* and *Richard III* represent its culmination. The *Life of John Picus* and the *Four Last Things*, which have received less consideration, are usually classified with the devotional works and studied more often for their biographical than for their literary significance. The literary position of the *Utopia* is undisputed—it is the masterpiece of

Renaissance humanism in England and the first book in the still-growing genre of utopian literature. It is admired as fiction, satire, and dialogue and claimed by thinkers of all dispositions—from conservative Catholics to socialist reformers. Moreover, scholars are still fascinated by all aspects of Utopian life—its family structure, government, economy, religion, philosophy. Although the *History of Richard III* is acclaimed for the unique contribution it makes to the development of English biography, history, and drama, it has been studied far less extensively than the *Utopia;* much of the scholarship on the *Richard* stresses the problems of authorship, composition, and genre.

During the years from 1520 - 1533 More devoted his literary talents exclusively to his polemical defense of the Church. These years reveal a marked deterioration in the quality of More's writing. Historians have often linked his defense of the Church with what they see as a reversion to conservatism, speaking of the More who cursed Luther and the More who wrote the *Utopia* as if they were two different people.

With the exception of the *Tyndale,* which is fine dialogue and fine fiction, and of some of the exempla in the later books, the polemical works do not compare well with the earlier works. At worst they are dull, strident, and verbose. At his polemical best, More uses dialogue, satire, and comedy to serve his controversial goals; even his prolix digressions serve a purpose at times. C. S. Lewis agrees with most critics that More's polemics are too often repetitious, but he defends the scurrilous humor as appropriate to the satiric tradition from which it derives: "It was More's business to appeal to the vulgar, to play to the gallery, and it suited one side of him extremely well. He is our first great cockney humorist, the literary ancestor of Martin Marprelate and Nashe. . . . It is when he is being serious that his abusiveness becomes a literary fault. To rebuke magnificently is one of the duties of a great polemical writer. More often attempts it but he always fails. He loses himself in a wilderness of opprobrious adjectives."[12] More's urgency is apparent as he seems increasingly to be trying to say everything against the heretics at once, and to an audience which he has come to think so dull and wrong-headed that it can be affected only by total bombardment.

Although there is no denying the flaws in More's controversial writing, it contains some of his best comic and fictional work. Because of the style of much of it and because of the subject matter, these books have received little consideration as literature. This is unfortunate, certainly in the case of the *Tyndale*, which is masterfully subtle both as fiction and as polemic. For its fictional use of dialogue and characterization it deserves careful scholarly consideration along with the *Utopia* and the *Dialogue of Comfort*. Nor have the polemical books yet received the attention they deserve in terms of what they tell us about the development of More's thought. There are, however, good reasons for the neglect: these books are not exciting reading for the modern scholar, and good modern editions are still not available for most of them.

The Tower works have fared a little better, but they too have failed to receive the serious scholarly treatment they deserve. They have often been read biographically in the light of More's martyrdom but seldom as the significant body of devotional literature they are. This is particularly unfortunate in the case of the *Dialogue of Comfort*, which in many ways represents the culmination of More's literary and spiritual development. The work of C. S. Lewis and R. W. Chambers and, more recently, of Louis L. Martz, Leland Miles, Frank Manley, Garry E. Haupt, and Clarence H. Miller has begun to attract critical attention to the Tower works.[13] Still, most modern writers follow the early biographers in stressing the circumstances that surrounded the composition of the last books: they were written, some of them perhaps with a piece of coal, by a man about to die for his faith. The emphasis continues to be on the saintliness rather than the artistry of the writer. Perhaps C. S. Lewis is right in saying that the ascetic and spiritual sides of More's character never found the perfect literary expression they merited.[14] Unfortunately, however, the artistry of the devotional literature he did write has been neglected.

III   *Conclusions*

Although the orientation of this study is more literary than biographical, the work of a man like Thomas More cannot be considered apart from his life. We have divided More's works into three periods characterized respectively by his involvement in humanism, his defense of the Church, and the time spent in the Tower. The analysis of More's writings suggests an answer to the question that has haunted all interpretations of his life: is More, the man and the writer, inexplicably contradictory or is he heroically whole, a saint? This study sees in More's works a process of maturation which allowed him to actualize various facets of his personality at different times. To put it in very modern terms, a chronological analysis of More's works shows him in the process of "creating himself." There is little reason to doubt that as a young man More was beset with the conflicts inherent in the personalities of complex persons, especially ones with the magnitude and variety of talents that he had. He was drawn to the active and the contemplative lives, to service in the Church, the monastery, and the state, as well as to the law and scholarship. Later, we see More using his diverse interests and talents in a way that orders the potential disorder of such profusion. His life presented a series of opportunities which enabled him to express his talents progressively and thus bring to fruition the diffuse promise of youth. He changes, not because he is confused, but because the times and circumstances call for the progressive use of his talents, never giving him an opportunity to develop one at the expense of the others, as Erasmus wanted him to do with his liberal studies and as C. S. Lewis wishes he had done with his devotional writings.[15] More was, in a literary as well as a spiritual sense, "a man for all seasons."

In his writing, we see clearly the chronological development, but there is also a constant overlapping and mingling of techniques and interests that suggests the original abundance and enriches everything. During the years of early maturity, from 1500 until about 1520, More was occupied with public life and writing his important humanist works—the poems, the translations of Lucian, the *Utopia*, the *History of Richard III*. But the *Life of John Picus* and the *Four Last Things* reveal the pervasively meditative aspect of More's thought, a potential which did not find full expression for many years.

His last fifteen years, filled with great disappointment as well as great success, bring the peak of More's political career. And this is the time that affords him the opportunity to express his theological and ecclesiastical concerns in defending the Church against the reformers. The controversial books show More applying the techniques he learned in the earlier period to his present purposes.

From about 1500, More was engaged in the active life, directing his energies toward trying to understand and improve the world in which he lived. The polemical years do not represent a change in More's goals; they give expression to a theological bent that had always been there. The polemics, the *Utopia*, and the *Richard* all have the same goal—to make Christendom the kind of place it should be but is not.

The Tower works and the devotional writings, however, reveal a different side of More's nature, the contemplative. But this too had always been there; it did not just surface as an escape for one disillusioned with the world and his own attempts to change it. The prison books express maturely the inclinations that we see in More's attraction to the Charterhouse, in his ascetic practices, and in the early devotional writing. More's persona admits in the *Utopia* that he does not expect perfection in humanity and society, not in this life (101, 247). In the Tower, More was able to do what he told his family, Henry VIII, and Erasmus he wanted to do—look toward that world where perfection is possible. Thomas More was a man of integrity and also a man of common sense; he applied himself where he was needed and followed the inclinations of persona More, who tells Hythlodaeus that the man with a "generous and truly philosophic spirit" should devote himself to the public interest and "perform as best he can whatever play is being performed" (99).

Notes and References

Chapter 1

1. Desiderius Erasmus, *Opus Epistolarum Des, Erasmi Roterodami,* ed. P. S. Allen and continued by H. M. Allen and H. W. Garrod (Oxford: Clarendon, 1906 - 1958), IV, No. 999. Hereafter cited as EE by volume and number of letter.

2. See Germain Marc'hadour, *L'Universe de Thomas More* (Paris: Librairie Philosophique J. Vrin, 1963), pp. 34 - 41; and R. W. Chambers, *Thomas More* (London: Jonathan Cape, 1935), p. 49.

3. Nicholas Harpsfield, *The Life and Death of Sir Thomas More,* ed. Elsie Vaughan Hitchcock, Early English Text Society, Original Series No. 186 (London: Oxford University Press, 1932), p. 12. EE, IV, No. 999.

4. Harpsfield, pp. 13 - 14.

5. William Roper, *The Lyfe of Sir Thomas Moore, knighte,* ed. Elsie Vaughan Hitchcock, Early English Text Society, Original Series No. 197 (London: Oxford University Press, 1935), p. 6. Roper's *Life* is our earliest biography of Thomas More. It was written in the early 1550s, about twenty years after More's death, but not printed until 1626.

6. Roper, p. 7. Thomas Stapleton, *The Life and Illustrious Martyrdom of Sir Thomas More,* trans. Philip E. Hallett, ed. E. E. Reynolds (New York: Fordham University Press, 1966), p. 25.

7. Roper, p. 7 - 8.

8. Thomas More, *The Correspondence of Sir Thomas More,* ed. Elizabeth Frances Rogers (Princeton: Princeton University Press, 1947), p. 36. Hereafter cited as *Correspondence. St. Thomas More: Selected Letters,* ed. Elizabeth Frances Rogers (New Haven and London: Yale University Press), pp. 17 - 18. Hereafter cited as *Selected Letters.*

9. Jane Colt had died by 1511. Shortly after her death More married Alice Middleton, who figures as Dame Alice in some of More's tales.

10. Harpsfield, pp. 65 - 66.

11. *Correspondence,* No. 3. *Selected Letters,* No. 2.

12. Paul Oskar Kristeller, *Renaissance Thought, The Classic, Scholastic, and Humanist Strains* (New York: Harper & Row, 1961), pp. 3 - 23.

13. Cresacre More, *The Life of Sir Thomas More* (London: William Pickering, 1828), pp. 27 - 28.

14. Roper, pp. 8 - 12. Harpsfield, p. 21. Stapleton, pp. 71 - 74.

15. EE, II, No. 388.

16. Roper, p. 10.

17. EE, III, No. 688.

147

18. EE, III, No. 829, No. 832. *Correspondence*, No. 57. *Selected Letters*, No. 18.

19. J. H. Hexter, "The Composition of *Utopia*," *The Complete Works of Sir Thomas More:* Vol. 4, *Utopia*, ed. J. H. Hexter and Edward Surtz, S.J. (New Haven and London: Yale University Press, 1965), pp.xv - xxiii. Hexter, *More's Utopia, the Biography of an Idea*, (1952; rpt. New York: Harper & Row, 1965). EE, II, No. 461. *Selected Letters*, No. 6.

20. *Correspondence*, No. 60. *Selected Letters*, No. 19.

21. *Correspondence*, No. 63, No. 101, No. 106, No. 107, No. 108, No. 128. *Selected Letters*, No. 20, No. 29, No. 31, No. 33, No. 35.

22. Roper, p. 9. Harpsfield, pp. 20 - 21. See also Hubertus Schulte Herbrüggen, "Some New Letters of St. Thomas More," *The Tablet*, 218 (July 4, 1964), 744 - 46. For the dating of More's diplomatic activities, 1515 - 1521.

23. Roper, pp. 16 - 20. Chambers, pp. 203 - 208.

24. *Selected Letters*, No. 45, p. 181.

25. Although the word "divorce" is usually used in connection with the situation that arose between Henry VIII and Catherine of Aragon, what Henry was actually seeking was an annulment. He contended that, because Catherine had first been married to his brother Arthur, the marriage between them was invalid—thus, he was not, and never had been, married to her—despite the papal dispensation which had allowed it. Henry needed a male heir and seems to have convinced himself that his wife Catherine's failure to produce one was his punishment for having married his brother's wife in opposition to the laws of God. He based his case on two biblical texts from Leviticus: "Thou shalt not uncover the nakedness of thy brother's wife: it is thy brother's nakedness" (Leviticus 18:16); and, "If a man shall take his brother's wife, it is an impurity: he hath uncovered his brother's nakedness; they shall be childless" (Leviticus 20:21). Against Henry's argument, however, there was the biblical duty of the brother-in-law to marry his deceased brother's wife: "When brethren dwell together, and one of them dieth without children, the wife of the deceased shall not marry to another; but his brother shall take her, and raise up seed for his brother" (Deuteronomy 25:5). For a comprehensive discussion of the legal aspects of the "divorce" see J. J. Scarisbrick, *Henry VIII* (1968; rpt. Berkeley and Los Angeles: University of California Press, 1972), pp. 163 - 240, *et passim*.

26. Roper, pp. 19 - 20.

27. *Correspondence*, No. 189. EE, X, No. 2659. *Selected Letters*, No. 44, No. 45.

28. Roper, pp. 9, 25.

29. Harpsfield, p. 21.

30. Ibid., p. 51.

31. Stapleton, p. 72. Philip E. Hallett's translation.

32. EE, III, No. 816, No. 829, No. 832. Chambers, p. 169.

33. Chambers, p. 236.

34. G. R. Elton, "Sir Thomas More and the Opposition to Henry VIII," in *Essential Articles for the Study of Thomas More*, ed. R. S. Sylvester and G. P. Marc'hadour (Hamden, Connecticut: Archon Books, 1977), p. 79 - 91. First published in *Bulletin of the Institute of Historical Research*, 41 (1968), 19 - 34, and in an earlier version in *Moreana*, 15 - 16 (1967), 285 - 303. And G. R. Elton, "Thomas More, Councillor," in *St. Thomas More: Action and Contemplation*, ed. Richard S. Sylvester (New Haven and London: Yale University Press for St. John's University, 1972), pp. 85 - 122.

35. Elton, "Councillor," p. 92.

36. John J. Scarisbrick, "Thomas More: The King's Good Servant," *Thought*, 52 (1977), 256.

37. Elton, "Councillor," pp. 109 - 11.

38. Elton, "Opposition," p. 90.

39. Scarisbrick, p. 265.

40. More, *Utopia*, pp. 99 - 101.

41. EE, III, No. 785.

42. John L. Scarisbrick, *Henry VIII* (Berkeley and Los Angeles: University of California Press, 1968), p. 110.

43. *Correspondence*, No. 160.

44. See Thomas More, *The Complete Works of St. Thomas More:* Vol. 8, parts 1, 2, 3, *The Confutation of Tyndale's Answer*, ed. Louis A. Schuster, Richard C. Marius, James P. Lusardi, and Richard J. Schoeck (New Haven and London: Yale University Press, 1973), pp. 11 - 12, 20 - 34, 483 - 85, 608, *et passim*. Chambers pp. 274 - 82.

45. Thomas More, *The Apologye of Syr Thomas More, Knyght*, ed. Arthur Irving Taft, Early English Text Society, Original Series No. 180 (London: Oxford University Press, 1930), pp. 131 - 35.

46. EE, X, No. 2659. *Selected Letters*, No. 44, pp. 172 - 73.

47. *Correspondence*, No. 189. *Selected Letters*, No. 45.

48. *Correspondene*, No. 198. Selected Letters, No. 52, p. 202.

49. EE, X, No. 2831. *Selected Letters*, No. 46, p. 182.

50. *Correspondence*, No. 206, p. 531.

51. Roper, pp. 55 - 56.

52. *Correspondence*, No. 192. *Selected Letters*, No. 47.

53. Roper, pp. 59 - 61.

54. *Correspondence*, No. 198, No. 199. *Selected Letters*, No. 52, No. 53.

55. Chambers, pp. 291 - 305, *Correspondence*, No. 200. *Selected Letters*, No. 54.

56. Chambers, p. 73.

Chapter Two

1. See *Utopia. Complete Works:* Vol. 4, pp. clxxxvii - clxxxviii.

2. EE, III, No. 635.

3. See Leicester Bradner and Charles Arthur Lynch, "Introduction," in

The Latin Epigrams of Thomas More (Chicago: University of Chicago Press, 1953), p. xii.

4. Hoyt Hopewell Hudson, *The Epigram in the English Renaissance* (1947; rpt. New York: Octagon Books, Inc., 1966), pp. 1 - 21.

5. Thomas More, *The Latin Epigrams of Thomas More*, ed. Leicester Bradner and Charles Arthur Lynch (Chicago: University of Chicago Press, 1953), p. 131. Hereafter the epigrams will be cited from this text by in the English translation of Bradner and Lynch.

6. EE, II, No. 461. *Selected Letters*, No. 6.

7. Hudson, pp. 49 - 58. Bradner and Lynch,, pp. xxix - xxxi.

8. Thomas More, *The Complete Works of St. Thomas More:* Vol. 3, part 1, *Translations of Lucian*, ed. Craig R. Thompson (New Haven and London: Yale University Press, 1974), pp. 3 - 9. Hereafter cited in the text. Also *Correspondence*, No. 5.

9. *Selected Letters*, No. 19, p. 99. *Correspondence*, No. 60, p. 116.

10. EE, I, No. 191.

11. Stapleton, p. 9.

12. Ernest Edwin Reynolds, *The Field is Won* (Milwaukee: The Bruce Publishing Company, 1968), pp. 44 - 45.

13. See Giovanni Pico della Mirandola, "Oration on the Dignity of Man," in *The Renaissance Philosophy of Man*, ed. Ernst Cassirer, Paul Oskar Kristeller, and John Herman Randall, Jr. (Chicago and London: University of Chicago Press, 1948), pp. 215 - 54.

14. Thomas More, *The English Works of Sir Thomas More*, ed. W. E. Campbell: Vol. 1 (London: Eyre and Spottiswoode, Ltd., 1931), p. 355. Hereafter cited in the text.

15. The best general study of More's *Life of Picus* is Margaret Powell Esmonde's unpublished doctoral dissertation; see Esmonde, " 'A Patterne of Life': A Critical Analysis of St. Thomas More's *Life of John Picus*," Diss. University of Miami 1971, pp. 180 - 84. See also Stanford E. Lehmberg, "Sir Thomas More's Life of Pico della Mirandola," *Studies in the Renaissance*," 3 (1956), 61 - 74.

16. See Lehmberg, 61 - 62.

17. R. W. Chambers, "The Continuity of English Prose from Alfred to More and his School," in *The Life and Death of Sir Thomas More* by Nicholas Harpsfield, pp. xlv - clxxiv.

18. Esmonde, p. 100.

19. Ibid., p. 91 - 123.

20. More, *Utopia*, pp. 161 - 81. Judith P. Jones, "The *Philebus* and the Philosophy of Pleasure in Thomas More's *Utopia*," *Moreana*, 31 - 32 (1971), 61 - 69.

21. Thomas More, *The Complete Works of St. Thomas More:* Vol. 2, *The History of King Richard III*, ed. Richard S. Sylvester (New Haven and London: Yale University Press, 1963). Hereafter cited in the text.

22. See Richard S. Sylvester, "Introduction," *The History of King Richard III*, pp. xvii - lxv.

23. Sylvester, pp. liv - lix, lxix.

24. See Paul Murray Kendall, *Richard the Third* (New York: W. W. Norton and Company, 1955), pp. 465 - 514. Here Kendall offers an objective assessment of Richard's reputation and the death of the princes. E. F. Jacob, *The Oxford History of England: The Fifteenth Century, 1399 - 1485* (1961; rpt. London: Oxford University Press, 1969), pp. 605 - 45.

25. Jacob, p. 645.

26. G. M. Trevelyan, *History of England: Vol 1, From the Earliest Times to the Reformation* (1926; rpt. Garden City, New York: Doubleday & Company, 1953), p. 349.

27. S. T. Bindoff, *Tudor England*, (1950; rpt. Baltimore: Penguin Books Ltd., 1974), p. 8.

28. Sylvester, pp. lxii - lxiii, lxvi.

29. Ibid., pp. lxiii - lxxx.

30. Chambers, "The Continuity of English Prose," pp. xlviii, clxv - clxvii. Chambers, *Thomas More*, pp. 115 - 17.

31. A. F. Pollard, "The Making of Sir Thomas More's *Richard III*." *Historical Essays in Honour of James Tait*, ed. J. G. Edwards, V. H. Galbraith, E. F. Jacobs (Manchester, 1933), pp. 223 - 38.

32. Sylvester, p. xcviii. Robert E. Reiter, "On the Genre of Thomas More's *Richard III*," *Moreana*, 25 (1970), 5 - 16.

33. Reiter, 9.

34. Leonard F. Dean, "Literary Problems in More's *Richard III*," *PMLA*, 58 (1943), 27.

35. See Lee Cullen Khanna's treatment of the women in *Richard III* in "No Less Real than Ideal: Images of Women in More's Work," *Moreana*, 55 - 56 (1977) 35 - 50.

36. Chambers, *Thomas More*, pp. 115 - 17. Chambers, "The Continuity of English Prose," pp. clxv - clxvii.

37. Pollard, 223 - 38.

38. Sylvester, pp. lxxx - civ. C. S. Lewis, *English Literature in the Sixteenth Century excluding Drama* (New York and Oxford: Oxford University Press, 1954), pp. 166 - 67.

39. Reiter, 5 - 16.

40. Thomas More, *The Complete Works of St. Thomas More: Vol. 4, Utopia*, ed. Edward Surtz, S.J., and J. H. Hexter (New Haven and London: Yale University Press, 1965). Hereafter cited in the text.

41. Hexter, "The Composition of *Utopia*," *The Complete Works of St. Thomas More: Vol. 4*, pp. xxvii - xli.

42. Hexter, "The Composition of *Utopia*," pp. xvi - xxiii. Hexter, *More's Utopia*.

43. EE, IV, No. 999.

44. See EE, II, No. 461. *Selected Letters*, No. 6; EE, II, No. 467. *Selected Letters*, No. 7; EE, II, No. 481. *Selected Letters*, No. 9; *Correspondence*, No. 28. *Selected Letters*, No. 10; EE, II, No. 502. *Selected Letters*, No. 12; *Correspondence*, No. 31. *Selected Letters*, No. 13:

EE, II, No. 474, No. 477, No. 484, No. 487, No. 491, No. 499, No. 508, No. 513, No. 530, No. 534, No. 537.

45. For the letters, see More, *Utopia,* pp. 2 - 45; 248 - 53.

46. This quotation is taken from the text of a lecture by Warren W. Wooden, originally delivered at Thomas More College Quincentennial Conference on February 10, 1978. The essay, entitled "A Reconsideration of the Pererga of Thomas More's *Utopia,*" will be included in "Selected Essays" from that conference.

47. Peter R. Allen, "*Utopia* and European Humanism: The Function of the Prefatory Letters and Verses," *Studies in the Renaissance,* 10 (1963), 106.

48. Robbin S. Johnson, *More's Utopia, Ideal and Illusion* (New Haven and London: Yale University Press, 1969), pp. 27 - 28.

49. Hexter, "The Composition of *Utopia,*" pp. xvi - xxiii.

50. Hexter, *More's Utopia,* p. 115.

51. C. S. Lewis, pp. 168 - 69.

52. Hexter, *More's Utopia,* p. 112.

53. Chambers, *Thomas More,* p. 155.

54. Andrew D. Weiner, "Raphael's Eutopia and More's *Utopia:* Christian Humanism and the Limits of Reason," *Huntington Library Quarterly,* 39 (1975), 16.

55. Hexter, *More's Utopia,* p. 136.

56. Ibid., p. 99 - 155.

57. David M. Bevington, "The Dialogue in *Utopia:* Two Sides to the Question," *Studies in Philology,* 58 (1961), 496 - 509.

58. Edward L. Surtz, S.J., *The Praise of Pleasure: Philosophy, Education, and Communism in More's Utopia* (Cambridge, Mass.: Harvard University Press, 1957), p. 182.

59. Bevington, 508.

60. W. J. Barnes, "Irony and the English Apprehension of Renewal," *Queens Quarterly,* 73 (1966).

61. Johnson, pp. 30 - 68.

62. Barnes, 373.

63. Johnson, p. 36.

64. Ibid., p. 65.

65. Chambers, p. 131 - 44.

66. Surtz, *Utopia,* "Introduction," pp. cliii - clxxi. *The Praise of Pleasure,* pp. 192 - 99, *et passim.*

67. Karl Kautsky, *Thomas More and his Utopia,* trans. H. J. Stenning (London: A. & C. Black, Ltd., 1927).

68. Russell Ames, *Citizen Thomas More and his Utopia* (Princeton: Princeton University Press, 1949).

69. Hexter, *More's Utopia.* Hexter, "*Utopia* and the Medieval," pp. xlv - l; "A Window to the Future: The Radicalism of *Utopia,*" pp. cv - cxxiv in *Utopia.*

70. More, *Responsio*, pp. 275 - 77. *Apologye*, pp. 79 - 97. *Dialogue of Comfort*, pp. 166 - 87.

71. See Elizabeth McCutcheon, "Thomas More, Raphael Hythlodaeus, and the Angel Raphael," *Studies in English Literature: 1500-1900*, 9(1969), 21 - 38.

72. Martin N. Raitiere, "More's *Utopia* and *The City of God*," *Studies in the Renaissance*, 22 (1973), 144 - 68.

73. Wayne A. Rebhorn, "Thomas More's Enclosed Garden: *Utopia* and Renaissance Humanism," *English Literary Renaissance*, 6 (1976), 141.

74. Rebhorn, 140 - 55.

75. Johnson, *More's Utopia: Ideal and Illusion*.

76. Ward Allen, "Hythloday and the Root of All Evil," *Moreana*, 31 - 32 (1971), 54. For the debate between Allen and Hexter concerning More's attitude toward capitalism, see also: J. H. Hexter, "Intention, Words, and Meaning: The Case of More's *Utopia*," *New Literary History*, 6 (1975), 529 - 41; Ward S. Allen, "The Tone of More's Farewell to *Utopia*: A Reply to J. H. Hexter," *Moreana*, 51, 1976, 108 - 18.

77. Warren W. Wooden, "Anti-Scholastic Satire in Sir Thomas More's *Utopia*," *Sixteenth Century Journal*, 8 (1977), 43.

78. A. R. Heiserman, "Satire in the *Utopia*," *PMLA*, 78 (1963), 163 - 74.

79. Harry Berger, Jr., "The Renaissance Imagination: Second World and Green World," *Centennial Review*, 9 (1965), 36 - 78.

80. Arthur F. Kinney, "Rhetoric as Poetic: Humanist Fiction in the Renaissance," *ELH*, 43 (1976), 413 - 43.

81. Surtz, *Utopia*, "Introduction," pp. cliii - clxxix.

82. Stapleton, p. 103.

83. More, *The English Works of Sir Thomas More*: Vol. 1. Hereafter cited in the text.

84. Nancy Lee Beaty, *The Craft of Dying, A Study in the Literary Tradition of the Ars Moriendi in England* (New Haven and London: Yale University Press, 1970).

85. Chambers, "The Continuity of English Prose," pp. cxxi - cxxxiv. More, *Confutation*, p. 37.

86. Joseph Burnes Collins, *Christian Mysticism in the Elizabethan Age* (1940; rpt. New York: Octagon Books, 1971), p. 38.

87. *Correspondence*, No. 43, No. 63, No. 69, No. 70, No. 76, No. 101, No. 106 - 108, No. 128. *Selected Letters*, No. 17, No. 20, No. 22, No. 23, No. 29, No. 31 - 33.

88. *Correspondence*, No. 3. *Selected Letters*, No. 2.

89. *Correspondence*, No. 28. *Selected Letters*, No. 10.

90. *Correspondence*, No. 37, No. 111. *Selected Letters*, No. 16.

91. *Correspondence*, No. 57. *Selected Letters*, No. 18.

92. EE, II, No. 388. *Selected Letters*, No. 5.

93. *Selected Letters*, No. 7, p. 76. EE, II, No. 467.

94. *Selected Letters*, No. 11, pp. 84 - 85. EE, II, No. 499.

154   THOMAS MORE

95. EE, II, No. 513; III, No. 623, No. 688, No. 706.
96. EE, II, No. 461; III, No. 620; IV, No. 1087, No. 1093, No. 1096, No.
1117, No. 1131, No. 1133, No. 1184, No. 1185; VII, No. 1817, No. 2052.
Correspondence, No. 86.
97. *Correspondence*, No. 15. *Selected Letters*, No. 4.
98. Correspondence, No. 48, No. 75, No. 84, No. 85.
99. *Selected Letters*. No. 26, p. 139.

Chapter Three

1. Thomas More, *The Complete Works of St. Thomas More:* Vol. 5,
parts 1, 2, *Responsio ad Lutherum*, ed. John M. Headley (New Haven and
London: Yale University Press, 1969). Hereafter cited in the text.
2. See Headley in *Responsio ad Lutherum*, pp. 760 - 74. Also, Richard
C. Marius, "The Problem of the Papacy," in *The Complete Works of St.
Thomas More:* Vol. 8, part 3, *The Confutation of Tyndale's Answer*, pp.
1294 - 1315.
3. *Correspondence*, No. 143.
4. *Correspondence*, No. 160.
5. Thomas More, *The English Works of Sir Thomas More*, ed. W. E.
Campbell: Vol. 2 (London: Eyre and Spottiswoode, Ltd., 1931). Hereafter
cited in the text,
6. See R. C. Marius, "Thomas More and the Early Church Fathers,"
Traditio, 24 (1968), 379 - 407.
7. Thomas More, *The Supplication of Souls*, ed. Sister Mary Thecla
(Westminster, Maryland: The Newman Press, 1950). Hereafter cited in the
text.
8. See More, *Utopia*, pp. 161 - 63, 167, 221 - 23.
9. Toss and turn.
10. More, *The Confutation of Tyndale's Answer*. Hereafter cited in the
text.
11. *Correspondence*, No. 190.
12. *Correspondence*, No. 190, p. 462.
13. More, *Apologye*. Hereafter cited in the text.
14. Thomas More, *The Workes of Sir Thomas More, wrytten in the
Englysh tonge* (London, 1557), pp. 929 - 1034. Hereafter cited in the text.
15. C. S. Lewis, pp. 173 - 74. Rainer Pineas, *Thomas More and Tudor
Polemics* (Bloomington and London: Indiana University Press, 1968), p.
217. Arthur Irving Taft, "Introduction," More's *Apolgye*, p.. xliv - xlvii.
16. More, *The Workes*, pp. 1035 - 1138. Hereafter cited in the text.
17. *Correspondence*, No. 194, p. 468. More's letter to Thomas Cromwell
(February 1533 or 1534) makes it clear that More wrote the *Answer* before
his imprisonment, not during it, as early scholars assumed.
18. See W. D. J. Cargill Thompson, "Who Wrote 'The Supper of the
Lord'?" *Harvard Theological Review*, 53 (1960), 77 - 91. W. Clebsch,

"More Evidence that George Joye Wrote the Souper of the Lorde," *Harvard Theological Review*, 55 (1962), 63 - 66.

19. Louis L. Martz, "Thomas More: The Sacramental Life," *Thought*, 52 (1977) 301 - 302.

20. Inflamed sore.

Chapter Four

1. Thomas More, *The Complete Works of St. Thomas More:* Vol. 13, *Treatise on the Passion, Treatise on the Blessed Body, Instructions and Prayers*, ed. Garry E. Haupt (New Haven and London: Yale University Press, 1976). Hereafter cited in the text.

2. *Selected Letters*, No. 48.

3. Germain Marc'hadour, *Thomas More et La Bible* (Paris: Librairie Philosophique J. Vrin, 1969), pp. 72 - 73, 80. Haupt, *Treatise*, p. xxxix.

4. Louis L. Martz, "Thomas More: The Tower Works," in *St. Thomas More: Action and Contemplation*, ed. Richard S. Sylvester (New Haven and London: Yale University Press, 1972), pp. 57 - 83. See also Louis L. Martz, "Thomas More: The Sacramental Life," *Thought*, 52 (1977), 300-18.

5. Thomas More, *The Complete Works of St. Thomas More:* Vol. 14, parts 1 and 2, *De Tristitia Christi*, ed. Clarence H. Miller (New Haven and London: Yale University Press, 1976). Hereafter cited in the text. This edition includes a facsimile of More's autograph, the Valencia manuscript; the Latin text; and Miller's English translation. An appendix contains the English translation by More's granddaughter Mary Basset from the text of Rastell's 1557 edition.

6. Miller, *De Tristitia*, p. 739.

7. Martz, "The Sacramental Life," 307 - 18.

8. Thomas More, *The Complete Works of St. Thomas More:* Vol. 12, *A Dialogue of Comfort against Tribulation*, ed. Louis L. Martz and Frank Manley (New Haven and London: Yale University Press, 1976). Hereafter cited in the text.

9. Leland Miles, ed., *A Dialogue of Comfort against Tribulation* by Saint Thomas More (Bloomington and London: Indiana University Press, 1965), pp. xiv - xvi.

10. *Correspondence*, No. 206. Of this letter Rastell says: "Whether this answere were written by Sir Thomas More in his doughter Ropers name, or by hym self is not certainely knowen" (*Workes*, 1434). The language is so characteristic of More that it is generally assumed that he either wrote the letter or that he and Margaret composed it together.

11. Philip E. Hallett, ed., *A Dialogue of Comfort against Tribulation* by Thomas More (London: Burnes, Oates and Washbourne Ltd., 1937), p. v.

12. See Robert P. Adams, *The Better Part of Valor: More, Erasmus, Colet, and Vives, on Humanism, War and Peace, 1496 - 1535*, (Seattle:

University of Washington Press, 1962), pp. 194 - 211, 237, 262 - 303, *et passim.*

13. See R. J. Schoeck, "Thomas More's 'Dialogue of Comfort' and the Problem of the Real Grand Turk," *English Miscellany,* 20 (1969), 23 - 37.

14. For other discussions of the meaning and structure of the *Dialogue of Comfort* see: Leland Miles, "The Literary Artistry of Thomas More: *The Dialogue of Comfort,"* *Studies in English Literature, 1500 - 1900,* 6 (1966), 7 - 33. Louis L. Martz, "The Design of More's *Dialogue of Comfort,"* *Moreana,* 15 - 16 (1967), 331 - 46. Judith Jones, "The Structure of Thomas More's *A Dialogue of Comfort,"* *Selected Papers: Shakespeare and Renaissance Association of West Virginia,* 2 (1978), 20 - 29. Joaquin Kuhn, "The Function of Psalm 90 in Thomas More's *A Dialogue of Comfort,"* *Moreana,* 22 (1969), 61 - 67. Louis L. Martz, "The Tower Works," in *Complete Works,* Vol. 12, pp. lvii - lxxxvi. Frank Manley, "The Argument of the Book," in *Complete Works,* Vol. 12, pp. lxxxvi - clxiv.

15. Thomas More, *Thomas More's Prayer Book,* ed. Louis L. Martz and Richard S. Sylvester (New Haven and London: Yale University Press, 1969), pp. 205 - 206.

16. Thomas More, *Complete Works,* Vol. 13, "A Devout Prayer," p. 229.

17. *Correspondence,* No. 194, No. 197. *Selected Letters,* No. 49, No. 51.

18. *Correspondence,* No. 198. *Selected Letters,* No. 52.

19. *Correspondence,* No. 199, p. 495. *Selected Letters,* No. 53, p. 209.

20. *Correspondence,* No. 199, p. 498. *Selected Letters,* No. 533, p. 212.

21. *Correspondence,* No. 207, No. 208, No. 217. *Selected Letters,* No. 58, No. 59, No. 65.

22. *Correspondence,* No. 200. *Selected Letters,* No. 54.

23. *Correspondence,* No. 202. *Selected Letters,* No. 56.

24. *Correspondence,* No. 205.

25. *Correspondence,* No. 211, p. 547. *Selected Letters,* No. 61, p. 242.

26. *Correspondence,* No. 214, p. 552. *Selected Letters,* No. 63, p. 247.

27. Chambers, "The Continuity of English Prose," in Harpsfield's *Life of More,* pp. xc - cxxxiv. Garry E. Haupt has further demonstrated More's position in the tradition of medieval devotional writing in *The Complete Works of St. Thomas More,* Vol. 13, pp. lxxxiii - cxxii.

28. Evelyn Underhill, *Mysticism,* rev. ed. (1930; rpt. Methuen and Co. Ltd., 1967), p. 201 - 204.

29. Roper, p. 55.

30. *Correspondence,* No. 202, p. 509. *Selected Letters,* No. 56, p. 225.

31. *Correspondence,* No. 214. *Selected Letters,* No. 63.

32. More, *Prayer Book,* pp. 205 - 206.

Chapter Five

1. Chambers, "The Continuity of English Prose," Harpsfield, pp. xlv - clxxiv.

2. Christopher Hollis, *Thomas More* (London: Sheed & Ward, 1934). E. E. Reynolds, *The Field Is Won*. Kark Kautsky, *Thomas More and His Utopia*.

3. See Gilbert Burnet, *History of the Reformation 1485 - 1547* (Oxford: Clarendon Press, 1865), p. 210. J. A. Froude, *History of England from the Fall of Wolsey to the Defeat of the Spanish Armada* (London: J.W. Parker and Son, 1856), I, pp. 344 - 45; II, pp. 73 - 74, 227. John D. Acton, *Historical Essays and Studies* (London: Macmillan & Co., 1907), pp. 30-31. Mandell Creighton, *Persecution and Tolerance* (London: Longmans, Green, and Co., 1903), pp. 107 - 108.

4. EE, IV, No. 999, No. 1233.

5. Chambers, *Thomas More*, pp. 360 - 61.

6. Robert Bolt, *A Man for All Seasons* (1960; rpt. New York: Random House, 1962), p. xi.

7. Chambers, "Continuity," Harpsfield, pp. liii - liv.

8. Chambers, *Thomas More*, p. 360.

9. James Mackintosh, *Miscellaneous Works* (London: Longman, Brown, Green and Longmans, 1846), I, pp. 412 - 13.

10. George E. B. Saintsbury, *Short History of English Literature* (1898; rpt. London: Macmillan Press, 1966), pp. 211 - 12.

11. Lewis, p. 180.

12. Ibid., p. 175.

13. Louis L. Martz, "Thomas More: The Tower Works." Also, "The Design of More's *Dialogue of Comfort*," *Moreana*, 15 - 16 (1967), 331 - 46. Leland Miles, *A Dialogue of Comfort Against Tribulation*; and "The Literary Artistry of Thomas More: *The Dialogue of Comfort*," *Studies in English Literature, 1500 - 1900*, 6 (1966), 7 - 33. Louis L. Martz and Frank Manley, "Introduction," *A Dialogue of Comfort Against Tribulation*, pp. xix - clxvii. Garry E. Haupt, "Introduction," *Treatise on the Passion, Treatise on the Blessed Body, Instructions and Prayers*, pp. xvii - clxxxiv. Clarence E. Miller, "Introduction," *De Tristitia Christi*, pp. 695 - 778/

14. Lewis, p. 181.

15. Erasmus in *Utopia*, p. 3. Lewis, p. 181.

Selected Bibliography

BIBLIOGRAPHIES

There is not a perfect bibliography on More for two reasons—from the past there is a mass of general, not necessarily scholarly, material that must be dealt with, and recent years have brought such a proliferation of serious More scholarship that bibliographers have not been able to keep up with it. None of the existing bibliographies solves both problems. For secondary literature, the best sources are the editions in the St. Thomas More Project: *The Complete Works of St. Thomas More*, New Haven and London: Yale University Press, in progress. Useful for primary material and early Moreana is *St. Thomas More: A Preliminary Bibliography of his Works and of Moreana to the year 1750* by R. W. Gibson and J. Max Patrick, New Haven and London: Yale University Press, 1961. Gibson and Patrick include a bibliography of Utopiana. Also useful for secondary material is Frank and Majie Padberg Sullivan's *Moreana, Materials for the Study of Saint Thomas More*, Los Angeles: Loyola University of Los Angeles, 1964 - 1971. This book was published in five sucessive volumes from 1964-1971. It contains Moreana for the devotee as well as the scholar.

PRIMARY SOURCES

1. Editions of More's Writings
The Workes of Sir Thomas More, wrytten in the Englysh tonge.London, 1557. This comprehensive volume edited by More's nephew William Rastell is the standard primary edition of More's English works although there are earlier texts of many of the works.
Omnia, quae huiusque ad manus nostras pervenerunt, Latina Opera. Louvain, 1565. This is the earliest collection of More's Latin works. Cited here in connection with the *Richard*.
The Correspondence of Sir Thomas More. Ed. Elizabeth Frances Rogers. Princeton, New Jersey: Princeton University Press, 1947. A collection of More's extant letters.
St. Thomas More: Selected Letters. Ed. Elizabeth Frances Rogers. New Haven and London: Yale University Press, 1961. A selection of More's most important letters, all in English.
Sir Thomas More: Neue Briefen. Ed. Hubertus Schulte Herbrüggen. Munster: Verlag Aschendorff, 1966. An edition of significant letters and documents not included in the *Correspondence*.
The Yale Edition of the Complete Works of St. Thomas More. Executive

Ed. Richard S. Sylvester. New Haven and London: Yale University
Press. Vol. 2, *The History of Richard III*. Ed. Richard S. Sylvester
(1963). Vol. 3, prt. 1, *Translations of Lucian*. Ed. Craig R. Thompson
(1974). Vol. 4, *Utopia*. Ed. Edward Surtz, S.J., and J. H. Hexter (1965).
Vol. 5, *Responsio ad Lutherum*. Ed. John M. Headly, trans. Sr. S.
Mandeville (1969). Vol. 8, *The Confutation of Tyndale's Answer*. Ed.
Louis A. Schuster, Richard C. Marius, James P. Lusardi, and Richard
J. Schoeck (1973). Vol. 12, *A Dialogue of Comfort Against Tribulation*.
Ed. Louis L. Martz and Frank Manley (1976). Vol. 13, *Treatise on the
Passion, Treatise on the Blessed Body, Instructions and Prayers*. Ed.
Garry E. Haupt (1976). Vol. 14, *De Tristitia Christi*. Ed. Clarence H.
Miller (1976). *Thomas More's Prayer Book*. Ed. Louis L. Martz and
Richard S. Sylvester (1969).

The following is a selection of editions of some works that have not yet
appeared in the *Yale Works*, which will supersede them.
The English Works of Sir Thomas More. Ed. W. E. Campbell and A. W.
Reed et al., 2 Vols. London: Eyre and Spottiswoode, 1931. Cited here
for the *Life of John Picus, The Four Last Things* and the *Dialogue
concerning Tyndale*.
The Apologye of Syr Thomas More Knyght. Ed. Arthur Irving Taft. Early
English Text Society. O.S. No. 180. London: Oxford University Press,
1930.
The Latin Epigrams of Thomas More. Ed. and trans. Leicester Bradner and
Charles Arthur Lynch. Chicago: University of Chicago Press, 1953.
The Supplication of Souls. Ed. Sr. Mary Thecla, S.C. Westminster
Maryland: The Newman Press, 1950.

2. The Letters of Desiderius Erasmus.
Opus epistolarum Des. Erasmi Roterodami. Ed. P. S. Allen et al., 12 vols.
Oxford: Clarendon Press, 1906 - 1958. Trans. F. W. Nichols, *The
Epistles of Erasmus from His Earliest Letters to His Fifty-First Year*, 3
vols. London: Longmans, Green and Co., 1901 - 1918. *The
Correspondence of Erasmus*. Toronto: University of Toronto Press,
1974 - , in progress. The letters of Erasmus are a primary source of in-
formation concerning More's life and writings.

SECONDARY SOURCES

1. Biographies
BRIDGETT, T. E. *The Life and Writings of Sir Thomas More*. London: Burns
& Oates, Ltd., 1891.
CHAMBERS, R. W. *Thomas More*. London: Jonathan Cape, 1935. This is the
definitive modern biography. Chambers takes the traditional view of
More's life, stressing his spirituality and devoting a disproportionate
amount of space to the last few years of his life.

HARPSFIELD, NICHOLAS. *The Life and Death of Sir Thomas More*. Ed. Elsie
Vaughan Hitchcock. Early English Text Society, O.S. No. 186. London: Oxford University Press, 1932. Written around 1557. Although
the book is hagiographic, it is the first formal biography in English and
the first complete biography of More. It takes into account More's
literary accomplishments and augments and sometimes corrects
Roper's memoir. This edition includes the *Rastell Fragments*, the rem-
nant of a *Life of More* by More's nephew and editor, William Rastell.
MAYNARD, THEODORE. *Humanist as Hero, The Life of Sir Thomas More*.
New York: The Macmillan Company, 1947.
REYNOLDS, ERNEST EDWIN. *The Field is Won, The Life and Death of Saint
Thomas More*. Milwaukee: Bruce Publishing Company, 1968.
ROPER, WILLIAM. *The Lyfe of Sir Thomas More, knighte*. Ed. Elsie
Vaughan Hitchcock. Early English Text Society. O.S. No. 197. Lon-
don: Oxford University Press, 1935. Modernized edition in *Two Early
Tudor Lives*. Ed. Richard S. Sylvester and Davis P. Harding. New
Haven and London: Yale University Press, 1962. Roper was More's
son-in-law. This is our earliest and most intimate account of More's life
and the source of much that we know. It was written in the early
1550s, about twenty years after More's death, but not printed until
1626.
ROUTH, E. M. G. *Sir Thomas More and His Friends, 1477-1535*. London:
Oxford University Press, 1934.
STAPLETON, THOMAS. *The Life and Illustrious Martyrdom of Sir Thomas
More*. Ed. E. E. Reynolds, trans. Philip E. Hallett. New York:
Fordham University Press, 1966. Also hagiography, Stapleton's book
did not appear until 1588 and therefore is not as significant historically
as Roper's and Harpsfield's but it contains a collection of More's letters
not previously in print.

2. General Studies—Books

ADAMS, ROBERT P. *The Better Part of Valor*. Seattle: University of
Washington Press, 1962. A study of the pacificism of More, Erasmus,
Colet, and Vives.
BOLT, ROBERT. *A Man for All Seasons*. New York: Random House, 1960.
Popular play based on More's life from Erasmus and Roper; contains
an excellent introductory essay on More as a "saint of selfhood."
ESMONDE, MARGARET POWELL. " 'A Patterne of Life': A Critical Analysis of
St. Thomas More's *Life of John Picus*." Diss. University of Miami,
1971. The best general study of the *Life of Picus*.
HEXTER, J. H. *More's Utopia, The Biography of an Idea*. 1952; rpt. New
York: Harper and Row, 1965. Excellent general interpretation, essen-
tial to an understanding of the composition of *Utopia*.
HUDSON, HOYT HOPEWELL. *The Epigram in the English Renaissance*. 1947;
rpt. New York: Octagon Books, Inc., 1966. Contains the best single
study of the *Epigrammata*.

JOHNSON, ROBBIN S. *More's Utopia: Ideal and Illusion*. New Haven and London: Yale University Press. 1969. A provocative interpretation of *Utopia*.

KAUTSKY, KARL. *Thomas More and His Utopia*. Trans. H. J. Stenning. London: A. & C. Black, Ltd., 1927. A detailed Marxist interpretation of *Utopia*.

PINEAS, RAINER. *Thomas More and Tudor Polemics*. Bloomington and London: Indiana University Press, 1968. Good general study of More's polemical writing.

SURTZ, EDWARD, S.J. *The Praise of Pleasure*. Cambridge, Mass: Harvard University Press, 1957. A consideration of the philosophy, education, and communism of *Utopia*; an essential study.

————. *The Praise of Wisdom*. Chicago: Loyola University Press, 1957. A commentary on the religion and morality of the *Utopia*; like the above, essential, although both books present More's thought from the perspective of his Catholicism.

SYLVESTER, RICHARD S., ed. *St. Thomas More: Action and Contemplation*. New Haven and London: Yale University Press, 1972. Contains four excellent essays: More and the law, the Tower works, More as Councellor, More's spirituality.

WILLOW, SISTER MARY EDITH. *An Analysis of the English Poems of St. Thomas More*. Nieuwkoop: B. De Graaf, 1974. A consideration of More's English poetry.

3. General Studies—Periodicals

BEVINGTON, DAVID M. "The Dialogue in *Utopia*: Two Sides to the Question," *Studies in Philology*, 58 (1961), 496 - 509. A perceptive investigation of authorial stance in the *Utopia*.

DEAN, LEONARD F. "Literary Problems in More's *Richard III*." *PMLA*, 58 (1943), 22 - 41. Considers More's narrative technique in terms of classical theory and irony.

ELTON, G. R. "Sir Thomas More and the Opposition to Henry VIII," *Moreana*, 15 - 16 (1967), 285 - 303. A careful historical account of More's involvement in the issue of the king's marriages.

GREEN, PAUL D. "Suicide, Martyrdom, and Thomas More," *Studies in the Renaissance*, 19 (1972), 135 - 55. A consideration of More's attitudes toward suicide and martyrdom as they are reflected in his writing.

HEISERMAN, A. R. "Satire in the *Utopia*," *PMLA*, 78 (1963), 163 - 74. Considers More's satiric intent and his unique application of the conventions of satire.

LEHMBERG, STANFORD E. "Sir Thomas More's Life of Pico della Mirandola," *Studies in the Renaissance*, 3 (1956), 61 - 74. A consideration of the alterations made in translation.

MARIUS, R. C. "Thomas More and the Early Church Fathers," *Traditio*, 24 (1968), 379 - 407. Treats the role of the scriptures and patristic writing in More's thought.

MARTZ, LOUIS L. "The Design of More's *Dialogue of Comfort*," *Moreana*, 15 - 16 *(1967), 331 - 46. A literary interpretation of the Dialogue.*

MILES, LELAND. "The Literary Artistry of Thomas More: *The Dialogue of Comfort*," *Studies in English Literature, 1500 - 1900*, 6 (1966), 7 - 33. A good general reading.

Moreana, Bulletin Thomas More. This quarterly is the best single source of current Morean scholarship.

POLLARD, A. F. "The Making of Sir Thomas More's *Richard III*," in *Historical Essays in Honour of James Tait*. Ed. J. G. Edwards et al. Manchester, 1933. An important general reading.

RAITIERE, MARTIN N. "More's *Utopia* and *The City of God*," *Studies in the Renaissance*, 20 (1973), 144 - 68. A provocative analysis of the structure of paradox in *Utopia* and its relationship to Augustine.

SURTZ, EDWARD L., S.J. "Logic in *Utopia*," *Philological Quarterly*, 29 (1950).

SYLVESTER, RICHARD S. "A Part of His Own: Thomas More's Literary Personality in his Early Works," *Moreana*, 15 - 16 (1967), 29 - 42. Traces the develoPment of More's multiplicity of viewpoint as a literary device.

WOODEN, WARREN W. "Anti-Scholastic Satire in Sir Thomas More's *Utopia*," *Sixteenth Century Journal*, 8 (1977), 29 - 45. An analysis of the character of Hythlodaeus both as reformer and as the object of anti-scholastic satire.

Index

(The works of More are listed under his name)

163